FLOYD CLYMER'S MOTORCYCLIST'S LIBRARY

THE
BOOK OF THE ARIEL

A COMPLETE GUIDE FOR OWNERS AND PROSPECTIVE PURCHASERS OF ARIEL MOTOR-CYCLES

DEALING WITH EVERY PHASE OF MOTOR-CYCLING, INCLUDING CHAPTERS ON DRIVING, LEGAL MATTERS, INSURANCE, COMPETITION RIDING, AND OVERHAULING

BY
G. S. DAVISON

FOURTH EDITION

1932

ANNOUNCEMENT

By special arrangement with the original publishers of this book, Sir Isaac Pitman & Son, Ltd., of London, England, we have secured the exclusive publishing rights for this book, as well as all others in THE MOTORCYCLIST'S LIBRARY.

Included in THE MOTORCYCLIST'S LIBRARY are complete instruction manuals covering the care and operation of respective motorcycles and engines; valuable data on speed tuning, and thrilling accounts of motorcycle race events. See listing of available titles elsewhere in this edition.

We consider it a privilege to be able to offer so many fine titles to our customers.

FLOYD CLYMER
Publisher of Books Pertaining to Automobiles and Motorcycles

2125 W. PICO ST.   LOS ANGELES 6, CALIF.

INTRODUCTION

Welcome to the world of digital publishing ~ the book you now hold in your hand, while unchanged from the original edition, was printed using the latest state of the art digital technology. The advent of print-on-demand has forever changed the publishing process, never has information been so accessible and it is our hope that this book serves your informational needs for years to come. If this is your first exposure to digital publishing, we hope that you are pleased with the results. Many more titles of interest to the classic automobile and motorcycle enthusiast, collector and restorer are available via our website at www.VelocePress.com. We hope that you find this title as interesting as we do.

NOTE FROM THE PUBLISHER

The information presented is true and complete to the best of our knowledge. All recommendations are made without any guarantees on the part of the author or the publisher, who also disclaim all liability incurred with the use of this information.

TRADEMARKS

We recognize that some words, model names and designations, for example, mentioned herein are the property of the trademark holder. We use them for identification purposes only. This is not an official publication.

INFORMATION ON THE USE OF THIS PUBLICATION

This manual is an invaluable resource for the classic motorcycle enthusiast and a "must have" for owners interested in performing their own maintenance. However, in today's information age we are constantly subject to changes in common practice, new technology, availability of improved materials and increased awareness of chemical toxicity. As such, it is advised that the user consult with an experienced professional prior to undertaking any procedure described herein. While every care has been taken to ensure correctness of information, it is obviously not possible to guarantee complete freedom from errors or omissions or to accept liability arising from such errors or omissions. Therefore, any individual that uses the information contained within, or elects to perform or participate in do-it-yourself repairs or modifications acknowledges that there is a risk factor involved and that the publisher or its associates cannot be held responsible for personal injury or property damage resulting from the use of the information or the outcome of such procedures.

WARNING!

One final word of advice, this publication is intended to be used as a reference guide, and when in doubt the reader should consult with a qualified technician.

PREFACE

IN this book the reader should find all he requires to enable him to keep his mount in perfect condition, and it is also hoped that he will derive considerable pleasure and interest from its perusal, for some of the recent Ariel models are obviously very clever engineering jobs, and a study of their design and construction is recommended to all interested in motor-cycling developments as well as to prospective buyers.

Special attention has been paid to that remarkable new model the "Square Four," which was received with such enthusiasm at the 1930 motor-cycle show at Olympia. This machine has an exceptional turn of speed and its general performance is well above normal.

For the benefit of the novice, the principles of the magneto, carburettor, and the four-stroke engine are fully explained in Chapter V. The reader, be he novice or expert, will find the general overhauling notes of special value, and the various sub-headings should enable him to refer quickly to any special point about which he desires to obtain information or verification.

CONTENTS

CHAP.		PAGE
	PREFACE	
I.	THE RANGE OF ARIEL MOTOR-CYCLES	1
II.	THE RUNNING COSTS OF AN ARIEL MOTOR-CYCLE	18
III.	THE LAW, LICENCES, INSURANCE	24
IV.	RUNNING-IN AND DRIVING HINTS	31
V.	THE FOUR-STROKE ENGINE	39
VI.	MAINTENANCE AND OVERHAULING	47
VII.	WHEELS AND TYRES	92
VIII.	PREPARING THE ARIEL FOR COMPETITIONS	97
IX.	USEFUL INFORMATION	108
	INDEX	109

THE BOOK OF THE ARIEL

CHAPTER I

THE RANGE OF ARIEL MOTOR-CYCLES

ONE of the oldest firms in the motor-cycle industry, Ariel Works, Ltd., has of late years concentrated on the production of medium-weight machines. This type of mount served a large number of motor-cyclists, but within the last year or two it was felt that the range could be advantageously expanded to meet the demands of the men and women who require a light, easily controlled machine at a very moderate price.

In 1929, therefore, the manufacturers introduced their 250 c.c. types, and last year added yet another small machine to their catalogue, in the form of a 350; 1931 also saw the production of the now famous " Square Four." The result is that, in 1932, the motor cycling public may choose from the Ariel catalogue all types of machines, ranging from a 250 c.c. side valve to a 600 c.c. edition of the Square Four.

The machines for 1932 are thirteen in number, and are classified and priced as follows—

		£	s.	d.
LB/32	250 s.v.	37	10	–
LF/32	250 o.h.v.	40	10	–
MB/32	350 s.v.	38	10	–
M1F/32	350 o.h.v.	40	10	–
M2F/32	350 o.h.v.	41	10	–
MH/32	350 o.h.v.	43	10	–
VB/32	550 s.v.	47	10	–
VG/32	500 o.h.v.	50	10	–
SB/32	550 s.v.	54	10	–
VH/32	500 o.h.v.	57	10	–
SG/32	500 o.h.v.	57	10	–
4F/5/32	500 o.h.c.	67	10	–
4F/6/32	600 o.h.c.	67	10	–

These prices do not include electric lighting or any extras.

Three types of sidecar are marketed, and these are known as model R standard touring, priced at £16; model U special touring, £18; and model W, special sports, £20.

At first sight the range appears to contain a redundancy of models, but in actual fact the machines are all of different types, although by careful standardization the makers have been able to use many of the same component parts in different models; in this way low prices follow as a natural consequence.

The specifications of the light-weight machines are in many respects similar. A full description, therefore, of the first model in the range, LB/32, to some extent covers several of the following machines.

Model LB/32. The first and lowest priced machine in the Ariel range, model LB/32, has the following specification.

ENGINE. The engine is of the single cylinder type with side-by-side valves, and running, of course, on the four-stroke principle. The bore is 65 mm., and the stroke 75 mm., giving a cubic

FIG. 1. THE 250 C.C. S.V. MODEL

capacity of 248 c.c., and the cylinder head is integral with the barrel. The connecting rod big-end bearing runs on double-row roller bearings, while ball bearings are fitted on either side of the mainshaft. A flat-topped piston made of heat-treated "L8" aluminium alloy is used, and the engine shaft carries a transmission shock absorber.

THE LUBRICATION SYSTEM. The engine is lubricated on the "dry sump" principle, which ensures a continuous mechanical oil circulation operated by a double plunger and scavenging pump. The oil is doubly filtered and is fed under pressure through the hollow timing spindle direct to the big-end bearing. From thence it is thrown on to the cylinder walls and little end, and, falling into the sump, is returned by the scavenging pump to the supply tank.

The system is entirely automatic and requires no adjustment. By removing the filler-cap of the oil tank it is possible to see the return and to judge if the oil supply is functioning correctly,

THE RANGE OF ARIEL MOTOR-CYCLES

although this can also be ascertained from an oil pressure gauge, which is mounted in the tank. This method of lubrication is now almost universal for motor-cycles; it ensures a low oil consumption and minimizes the possibility of over-oiling or oiling-up the

FIG. 2. THE 250 C.C. O.H.V. MODEL

FIG. 3. THE 550 C.C. VERTICAL S.V. MODEL

sparking plugs. On a 25 m.p.h. basis, one pint of oil is circulated through the engine every 10 minutes, and the average oil consumption of an LB/32 machine is approximately 4,000 m.p.g.

To keep the oil cool the crankcase has deep external cooling fins, while a feature of Ariel machines is the fitting of a centrifugal oil purifier in the fly-wheel. Centrifugal force throws the oil as it passes down a passage in the fly-wheel to the circumference, where any impurities are trapped and can later be removed by the detachment of a screwed plug.

CARBURETTOR. On the "L" models, the Amal instrument is clipped to a short induction pipe, and is not flange-fitted as on the rest of the range. It is provided with a throttle stop to make a "tick-over" setting, variable independently of the cable adjustment. The air slide is controlled by a handlebar lever, whilst the throttle has twist-grip control.

MAGNETO. A Lucas magneto is standardized and is mounted

FIG. 4. THE 500 C.C. VERTICAL FOUR-VALVE MODEL

on a platform situated between the seat pillar and the sloping cylinder. It is driven by an enclosed chain running in an aluminium case, fully lubricated. Purchasers are given the option of a Maglita or a Magdyno instrument, if electric lighting is ordered. Both instruments are priced at nearly the same figure, but if the Maglita is used the machine weighs less than 224 lb., and is, therefore, eligible for the 30s. tax.

EXHAUST SYSTEM. The exhaust pipe runs into a large expansion chamber, which is situated below the rear wheel spindle on the offside. The expansion chamber, fitted with baffles and a fishtail, gives an exceptionally quiet note.

TRANSMISSION. This is carried out by Coventry chains through a three-speed Burman gear box. The front chain is of $\frac{1}{2}$ in. × ·305 in. dimensions, while the rear chain is $\frac{5}{8}$ in. × $\frac{3}{8}$ in. Both chains are automatically lubricated and the primary drive is enclosed in an aluminium oil bath.

GEAR BOX. This is especially designed and manufactured by Messrs. Burman & Sons, Ltd. The gear box pivots on a top anchorage for primary chain adjustment, and is provided with speedometer drive.

THE RANGE OF ARIEL MOTOR-CYCLES

FRAME. The same type of frame is used for all the lightweight machines, and it is, therefore, designed upon particularly robust lines. It is of the open type and from a one-piece steel head lug are arranged two top tubes and a front down tube of $1\frac{1}{2}$ in. diameter. All the main tubes are of Aero quality steel and all are straight. The top tubes run to a seat pillar lug, into the rear ends of which are brazed the back forks. The base of the front down tube carries engine plates and the rear engine plates are bolted to a duplex seat pillar. This frame gives a very low riding

FIG. 5. THE 550 C.C. SLOPING S.V. MODEL

position and is famous in the trials world for its excellent steering qualities and weight distribution.

BRAKES. The design of the brakes used on Ariel machines is in accordance with modern motor-car practice. On the LB/32 both front and rear brakes are $5\frac{1}{2}$ in. in diameter, and operate on the internal-expanding principle. The brake shoes are of aluminium fitted with die-pressed linings. Dual, internal coil springs are used to return the shoes, and quick hand adjustment is provided for both brakes. The wheels run on taper roller bearings, have well-base rims with heavy weight spokes, and carry 25 in. × 3 in. wired-on Dunlop tyres.

SUSPENSION. Suspension is provided at the rear by a spring seat saddle, which is adjustable for height. The front wheel is sprung on Ariel-made forks with a central barrel-type coil spring working in tension. Friction discs are used on the fork links, whilst a steering damper can be obtained as an extra. The forks, in common with the other cycle parts, may be lubricated when necessary by means of a grease gun supplied with the tool kit.

TANK. The saddle tank, which fits over and conceals the top tubes, is chromium-plated with a black enamel panel on top to prevent sun dazzle. It is capable of carrying 2 gallons of fuel, and the large diameter, quick action filler cap is located to balance the speedometer, if one is fitted. The oil pressure gauge, previously mentioned, completes this arrangement and lies flush with the tank top. The gear lever gate and pneumatic knee grips

FIG. 6. THE 500 C.C. "RED HUNTER"

are fitted to the tank sides. The separate welded steel oil tank, mounted on the saddle pillars, contains submerged strainers.

MISCELLANEOUS. The specification of the Model LB/32 Ariel is completed by wide mudguards (the front being plain and the rear having a detachable section to facilitate wheel removal), a spring-up rear stand, adjustable footrests, adjustable handlebars of a sporting pattern, a tool box containing a complete set of tools, and a grease gun.

It is interesting to note that the handlebars are of the " clean " type, but, if preferred, ordinary clip-on controls may be fitted without extra cost.

Model LF/32. This model has a specification similar to the LB/32, except as regards the engine. This is of the two-port o.h.v. type, with a detachable cylinder head. The rockers are carried on stout plate supports and double valve springs are employed. The push rods and rockers are enclosed and the inlet

THE RANGE OF ARIEL MOTOR-CYCLES 7

valve guide is lubricated directly from the crank case. Tappet adjustment is made at the base of the push rods, the nuts being enclosed in a small compartment cast on the base of the cylinder barrel and protected by an aluminium cover.

Models MB/32, M1F/32, and M2F/32. These three machines are all of 350 c.c. and their general specification, with the exception of the engines, is much the same as that of the " L " models. Model M2F/32, however, differs again in that the brakes are of

FIG. 7. THE 500 C.C. SLOPING O.H.V. MODEL

$6\frac{1}{2}$ in. diameter and 25 in. × 3·25 in. tyres are used. Further, the Maglita instrument is not fitted to this machine and it carries a steering damper as standard. The models MB and M1F, like the " L " models, are taxable at 30s. per year if fitted with a Maglita.

Model MB has a sloping side valve engine with a detachable cylinder head of special design. The bore and stroke measurements are 72 mm. × 85 mm. respectively, giving a capacity of 348 c.c. The valve gear is totally enclosed and automatically lubricated, while the crank case details are similar to those of the " L " machines. M1F has the same bore and stroke dimensions and capacity, but the cylinder head has a single o.h.v. exhaust port, while M2F is a two-port mount.

There is yet another 350 in the range—MH/32, a special sporting machine, which will be described later in conjunction with its prototype of 500 c.c.

Models VB/32 and VG/32. These two machines have vertical engines and are identical in specification, except that one has overhead valves and the other side valves. The following specification, therefore, will cover both machines.

8 THE BOOK OF THE ARIEL

ENGINE. The side valve machine has a bore and stroke of 86·4 × 95 mm., the total cubic capacity being 557 c.c., whilst that of the o.h.v. model is 499 c.c. (86·4 mm. × 85 mm.). The VG has a two-port head incorporating four valves. Tappet adjustment is carried out by setting the individual rockers. The o.h.v. gear is, of course, enclosed and lubricated. As on the smaller models, the big end has double-row roller bearings, and ball bearings are fitted on the driving and timing sides of the

FIG. 8. THE FOUR-CYLINDER MODEL

main shaft. The engine's lubrication is on the dry sump principle already described.

GEAR BOX. The three-speed gear box is especially designed and manufactured by the Burman concern for Ariel machines; it is mounted with bottom-fixing and top anchorage and draw-bolt chain adjustment. A hand-operated, four-plate fabric insert clutch, with a rubber shock-absorbing device in the clutch housing is fitted.

TRANSMISSION. The primary chain is enclosed by a sheet steel chain case incorporating a chain oiling device. The rear chain is protected by very efficient guards both on the top and bottom runs.

PETROL TANK. This is of welded steel, the capacity being $2\frac{1}{2}$ gallons. It is fitted with a fuel strainer and a two-level cork-seated petrol tap, allowing for a reserve supply.

BRAKES. The brakes on these two models, as on the remaining machines, are 7 in. in diameter, and have the new fulcrum adjustment. That is to say, wear of the linings may be taken up in either of two ways: (1) in the normal manner, by adjusting the cable or operating rod; and (2) by a device which extends the

THE RANGE OF ARIEL MOTOR-CYCLES

Fig. 9. Standard Touring Model

Fig. 10. Special Touring Model

shoes at the pivoting point. This system makes for a more even pressure of the shoes on the drums, increases braking efficiency, and reduces wear of the linings.

MISCELLANEOUS. Front and rear stands are fitted, the latter being of the spring-up type, and the finish is in the best black enamel with all the bright parts, including the tank, chromium-plated. The petrol filler, speedometer (if fitted), and oil gauge are all arranged flush in the tank top.

Models VH/32 and MH/32. These two models are late editions to the 1932 range and are special competition mounts, introduced to meet the demands of the sporting rider who wishes to combine fast road or trials work with occasional racing. They bear the name " Red Hunter " on the tank and have a particularly sporting appearance as well as performance. A description of the 500 c.c. machine will be given first.

ENGINE. A vertical engine, specially tuned for high speed work, is employed, the dimensions being 86·4 × 85 mm. and capacity 499 c.c. The detachable cylinder head is of the two-port type and carries four valves. The inlet valves are lubricated by suction from the crank case and are fitted with double valve springs; the valve gear is totally enclosed. The fly wheels, connecting rod, cylinder head, and ports are highly polished and alternative pistons are supplied. Either piston may be used to suit the particular requirements of the rider. The compression ratio with the standard piston (with which the machine is fitted when delivered) is 6 to 1, and, with the high compression piston, 7·5 to 1. The engine is lubricated on the usual Ariel dry-sump principle, and the arrangement of the big end and main bearings is the same.

GEAR BOX. The " Red Hunter " has a specially close ratio three-speed Burman box, operated by foot and having ratios of 5, 7·5, and 10·4 to 1. The clutch has four fabric insert plates.

CARBURETTOR. This is a large bore Amal instrument, flange fitted, and connected to the tank by means of a Petroflux supply pipe.

MAGNETO. A Lucas racing magneto is supplied as standard, or a Lucas Magdyno if the machine is ordered with electric lighting.

FRAME. The frame is of the open cradle type, as used on the VB and VG models, and is fitted with two sets of footrests, one pair in the normal position and one on the rear chain stays. The forks are also the same as those used on all medium-weight machines and have a central barrel compression spring, shock absorbers, and a steering damper.

WHEELS. The brakes are 7 in. in diameter and have the new

THE RANGE OF ARIEL MOTOR-CYCLES 11

fulcrum adjustment. Dunlop 26 in. × 3 in. and 26 in. × 3·25 in. tyres are fitted on the front and rear wheels respectively, the former being ribbed and the latter studded. The rims are chromium-plated with red centres, and narrow C-section mudguards are used. The rear guard has a split portion to facilitate the rear wheel removal, and is fitted with a back cushion.

MISCELLANEOUS. A feature of the machine is the high level arrangement of the exhaust pipes and Carbjector silencers. The petrol tank has a capacity of 2½ gallons and is finished in chromium with a red top panel, incorporating a speedometer aperture, quick

FIG. 11. SPECIAL SPORTS MODEL

release filler cap, and oil pressure gauge. Handlebars with a road-racing bend and clip-on controls are fitted, and the equipment is completed by a chain stay tool box.

The 350 c.c. Red Hunter has as its basis the specification of the M2F model already described, together with the red and chrome colour scheme, high level exhaust pipes, tyre sizes, close ratio gear box, specially tuned, high compression engine, and additional footrests, etc., of the 500 c.c. model. Foot control is not available on this machine, nor is the fulcrum brake adjustment.

Models SB/32 and SG/32. These two machines are now generally known as the "Slopers," on account of the fact that the engines are set in the frame at the distinctly inclined angle of 30 degrees with the horizontal.

ENGINE. The side valve unit has dimensions of 86·4 × 95 mm., the capacity being 557 c.c. A large expansion chamber is situated under the cylinder, in front of the base of the down tubes, and from it two exhaust pipes lead to a pair of silencers, one on either side of the rear wheel. The arrangement is known as triple silencing.

The cylinder head is detachable, and the rest of the engine details, such as lubrication, bearings, etc., follow on the lines of those previously described. The side valve model is intended as a *de luxe* touring machine, particularly for use with a sidecar.

The o.h.v. version has a bore of 86·4 mm. and a stroke of 85 mm., giving a capacity of 499 c.c., and the engine is specially tuned for high-speed work. It has a four-valve, two-port, detachable cylinder head, and the inlet valves are lubricated by suction from the crank case.

FRAME. The frame is of the duplex cradle type, being immensely strong and at the same time giving a remarkably low riding position.

GEAR BOX. This is a Burman four-speed with provision for speedometer drive, and is controlled by a spring blade gear lever mounted on the tank side.

MISCELLANEOUS. A speedometer and an illuminated instrument panel, containing also an oil pressure gauge, filler cap, and receptacle for a clock are fitted as standard, whilst the primary chain is totally enclosed in an aluminium oil bath. A particularly handsome tank, capable of containing $3\frac{1}{8}$ gallons, is a feature, special kneegrips adding greatly to its appearance. Valanced mudguards, both front and back, are used, and the machine is fitted with two tool boxes.

Models 4F5/32 and 4F6/32. These two models are the 500 and 600 versions of the Square Four machine which was introduced at the 1930 Motor-cycle Show in its 500 c.c. form. The design is unique and represents the most advanced motor-cycle practice. In spite of this, the price is moderate. The machine is neat and compact, easily controllable, and has tremendous acceleration and a truly remarkable top gear performance, particularly as regards smooth running at low speeds.

The engine, which is little bigger externally than a single cylinder 500 c.c. unit, is neatly housed in a normal type of frame, and the whole lay-out can justly be described as a triumph of motor-cycle engineering. The specification follows, but the details concerning the magneto, silencers, gear box, tyres, brakes, instrument panel, and tank are the same as those outlined in connection with the " slopers."

ENGINE. This is a four-cylinder unit, having a bore and stroke of 51 mm. × 61 – 497 c.c., and, in the case of the 600, 55 mm. × 61 mm. – 597 c.c. It is designed on an entirely new principle, having twin, gear-coupled crankshafts mounted on large diameter ball bearings. The main coupling gears, of specially developed tooth form, are enclosed in a separate oil-fed chamber within the crank case. The light, high-tensile steel connecting rods have substantial roller bearing big-ends. The half-time shaft, which drives both the overhead camshaft and the magneto by specially tensioned roller chains, is operated by hardened and ground gears from the forward crankshaft.

The cylinders are cast *en bloc* and are designed to overcome distortion and to enjoy adequate and equal cooling. The easily

FIG. 12. INSTRUMENT PANEL

detachable cylinder head carries the exhaust passages and an ingenious radial induction manifold integral with the casting. The vertical overhead valves are operated by the camshaft directly through rockers, and the whole valve arrangement is totally enclosed in an aluminium casting, with a readily removable lid to enable the rider to reach the tappets.

The cam box is spigoted on to the cam chain case to prevent oil leakage.

LUBRICATION. The lubrication system employs two gear pumps and is of the dry sump type. Oil is pumped from the reservoir, which is a separate compartment at the rear of the crank case, and is first forced into the chamber enclosing the main crank shaft gears. From thence the oil overflows into troughs, and is picked up by dippers on the big-ends. The remainder of the internal moving parts of the engine are lubricated by oil mist, whilst a separate lead from the supply pump is taken to the overhead cam shaft and rocker box. The scavenging pump returns all surplus oil back to the reservoir.

CARBURETTOR. This is of the Amal flange fitted type, mounted forward of the block between the two exhaust pipes; it has twist-grip throttle and handlebar lever air control. Information con-

FIG. 13. THE REAR BRAKE FITTED ON 500-550 C.C. MODELS

cerning the tuning and maintenance of the carburettor is given in a later chapter.

MAGNETO. This instrument, which is manufactured by Lucas, is mounted behind the engine, and is thus protected from mud and dust which may be thrown up by the front wheel.

SILENCERS. Twin exhaust pipes, each dealing with two cylinders, lead to twin, stream-lined silencers on either side of the rear wheel. The exhaust note is extremely quiet; in fact exceptional silence, without loss of power through back-pressure, is a feature of these machines.

GEAR BOX. A four-speed Burman box, designed expressly for

the Square Four, is used. Chain adjustment is brought about by swivelling the box around its bottom anchorage. A hand-operated four-plate clutch, incorporating a shock absorber, is used, and the primary chain runs in an aluminium oil bath.

FRAME. This is of the duplex cradle type, built of solid steel forgings and Aero quality tubing. It is almost identical in design with the frames used for the SB and SG machines.

MISCELLANEOUS. The brake pedal is mounted on the near side to enable a foot change lever to be substituted for the tank

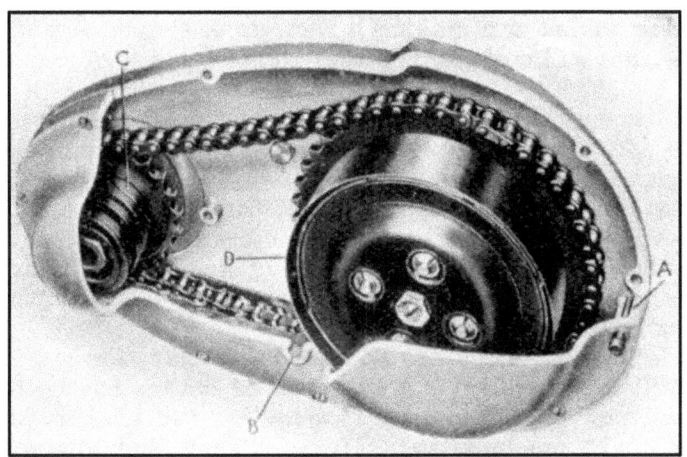

FIG. 14. OIL BATH CHAIN CASE
(All Models, except VB, VH, and VG)

control, if desired. A Magneto cut-out is provided and the Smith's trip-type speedometer has a 100 m.p.h. dial.

LIGHTING. Earlier in this chapter the prices of Ariel machines have been given. There are, however, a number of extras which are obtainable, and the most important of these is the Lucas Magdyno electric lighting set. For a solo machine, this set, complete with tail lamp, costs £5 10s., or £5 15s. if the instrument panel is illuminated; for a sidecar outfit the price in each case is 10s. more. The Maglita instrument and lighting equipment, which may be fitted to the lightweight machines to bring them within the 30s. tax limit, is priced at £5 5s.

Ariel Sidecars. The prices of Ariel sidecars have also been mentioned, but a brief review of the types will enable the reader to understand what the complete Ariel range offers to him.

The Ariel Chassis. The sidecar chassis is triangular in shape and is constructed of exceedingly strong tubes and massive lugs. It is attached to the machine by two large ball joints, one from the rear wheel lug and the other from the front engine plates in the case of the cradle frame machines, and from a special lug on the duplex cradle models.

Fine adjustment of alignment can be obtained by movement of the rear connection. The angle of the machine can then be varied by means of a connecting arm anchored below the saddle and attached to the sidecar chassis by a spring loaded connection. When the relative positions of the machine and sidecar are correct, the ball joints can be locked up, making a really firm attachment, which, however, will give just sufficiently for pleasant riding, the spring loaded arm making a very small degree of movement possible, but still maintaining that rigidity which sidecar drivers seek.

If it becomes necessary to remove the sidecar at any time, no trouble should be experienced in putting it back, for, once set, the alignment remains correct.

The sidecar body is suspended on three springs, and all the shackles are fitted with grease gun lubrication nipples. A pair of C-springs suspend the rear of the body, and the front is mounted on a long leaf spring. The hub bearings are of the taper roller type and are, of course, adjustable.

Readers of this book are advised to fit only sidecars of Ariel make to their machines, for this type of chassis has been specially designed to suit Ariel motor-cycles, and the use of other chassis might not only make fitting difficult, but might impose undue strains both on the motor-cycle frame and on the chassis itself.

Model R, Standard Touring. This sidecar is distinctive in design and is exceedingly comfortable. A hinged back cushion gives access to a very spacious locker. Only the finest leather cloth upholstery is used, while the body is finished in black fabric or polished aluminium. An all-weather hood meets a neat screen and forms a very cosy interior.

Model U, Special Touring. This is a model of very pleasing appearance, embodying pressed panels and a water-tight apron integral with the windscreen. The body is finished with cellulose in two colours. The prime colour is black, while " louvres " on the " bonnet " and the rear locker are finished in ivory.

Model W, Special Sports. This has a body finished in polished aluminium. It is of a very high standard of quality and has most graceful lines. It is designed to meet the wishes of those who require a sidecar embodying super-sports appearance with touring comfort.

For a sports body, it has unusual width and leg room, whilst

THE RANGE OF ARIEL MOTOR-CYCLES

the locker is capable of carrying a large amount of luggage. The pneumatic seat is of the hammock type, and the windscreen and apron give the occupant protection from the weather.

The various Ariel models have now been described as briefly as possible, but before turning to the more interesting subject of overhead and running costs, we will conclude this chapter with a summary of Ariel machines—

Model	c.c.	Bore and Stroke	Gear Ratios	Tyres (in.)	Tax
LB	250	65 × 75	17·0, 10·4, 6·4	25 × 3	30s.
LF	250	65 × 75	16·0, 10·0, 6·0	25 × 3	30s.
MB	350	72 × 85	15·2, 9·3, 5·7	25 × 3	30s.
M1F	350	72 × 85	14·4, 8·8, 5·4	25 × 3	30s.
M2F	350	72 × 85	14·4, 8·8, 5·4	25 × 3¼	£3
MH	350	72 × 85	10·3, 7·0, 5·4	26 × 3F	
				26 × 3¼R	£3
VH	500	86·4 × 85	10·4, 7·5, 5·0	26 × 3F	
				26 × 3¼R	£3
VB	550	86·4 × 95	13·8, 7·7, 4·75	26 × 3¼	£3
VG	500	86·4 × 85	13·8, 7·7, 4·75	26 × 3¼	£3
SB	550	86·4 × 95	12·6, 7·9, 5·9, 4·7	26 × 3¼	£3
SG	500	86·4 × 85	13·8, 8·6, 6·5, 5·2	26 × 3¼	£3
4F/5	500	51 × 61	15·3, 9·3, 7·2, 5·75	26 × 3¼	£3
4F/6	600	55 × 61	13·8, 8·6, 6·5, 5·2	26 × 3¼	£3

CHAPTER II

THE RUNNING COSTS OF AN ARIEL MOTOR-CYCLE

FOR motor-cycling to be a really enjoyable pastime it is of primary importance that its expense should be within the rider's means. This may seem obvious, but it is remarkable how many people buy machines which they ultimately find they cannot afford to run; after a few months' use, therefore, they are compelled to sell them, sometimes at a very low figure, since cash has become

FIG. 15. ARIEL RIDERS ENJOYING A PICNIC

immediately necessary to meet debts or household expenses. Many other would-be riders err on the side of over-estimating running costs, and therefore refrain from the purchase of a motor-cycle when they have actually the means necessary to the pastime.

The prospective purchaser can at once say whether or not he can afford to *buy* a motor-cycle. It is not so easy, however, for him to decide whether he can afford to run it. In this chapter, therefore, the costs of running and upkeep are carefully considered, so that those who contemplate becoming motor-cyclists can tell at once how much the first year's running should cost them. Subsequent years' costs can be calculated on a similar basis.

RUNNING COSTS OF AN ARIEL MOTOR-CYCLE

It is not possible here to include more than one example, as the space available is somewhat limited. The model "VG 32" is therefore selected, details being given as to both its solo and sidecar expenses. If the differences in the original cost, petrol consumption, etc., of other models be taken into consideration, it will be easy to arrive at the probable running costs of any Ariel motor-cycle or sidecar combination.

Overheads and Mileage Costs. The actual expenses must be considered under two separate headings—standing costs, or overheads, and actual running costs. The overheads are generally the heavier, unless the motor-cycle is used extensively, and they will therefore be taken first.

Overheads include interest on capital, depreciation, the annual tax, the driving licence, insurance, and garage rent—in fact, all items which vary but little, if at all, whether the machine is driven 1,000 or 20,000 miles during the year. Apart from depreciation, they can be assessed accurately at the beginning of the year. Depreciation, however, cannot be gauged exactly, since it depends partly on the mileage covered and the attention given to the machine, and partly on the owner's ability to find a prospective purchaser.

Depreciation. Some figure must, however, be taken, and for purposes of arriving at the overhead costs depreciation is considered to be at the rate of $33\frac{1}{3}$ per cent per annum, this to include a sum for loss of interest on capital. This means that a solo model "VG32" Ariel, equipped with a dynamo lighting set, speedometer and electric horn—a total cost of £59 2s. 6d.—is reckoned to be worth £39 8s. 4d. only after twelve months' use, depreciation being £19 14s. 2d. Provided that the machine is carefully kept and is not driven an excessive distance, the allowance may be said to be on the generous side.

What Constitutes Running Costs. The actual running expenses are easy to calculate. They include, in the main, the cost of petrol, oil, grease, tyres, and repairs. An allowance must be made for "bad luck" in respect of the two latter items. A tyre, for instance, may be badly cut early in its life and rendered useless, whilst one rider may be more unfortunate than another as regards the repairs and overhauls which become necessary. This depends largely, apart from luck, on driving ability, and a general average only can be taken. Washing and polishing are not included under running costs, since the majority of motor-cyclists clean their machines themselves.

In the case of the solo machine depreciation has been fixed at

£19 14s. 2d. A comprehensive insurance policy costs something like £6, tax is £3, and driving licence 5s. Garage can be neglected, since a solo machine can be stored in any passage or entry; if, however, the rider has no facilities for this, he will have to add the price charged by the local garage. The total overheads, then, are as follows—

	£	s.	d.
Depreciation	19	14	2
Insurance	6	0	0
Tax	3	0	0
Licence		5	0
	£28	19	2 per annum.

A model " VG 32 " machine fitted with an " R " sidecar, electric lighting set, and an electric horn costs £75 12s. 6d. Depreciation will therefore be £25 4s. 2d. Insurance will also cost approximately 2s. more, since there is a small additional charge if the value of the machine exceeds £50. The sidecar machine will in most cases have to be garaged elsewhere than on the owner's premises, the cost of this being approximately 2s. 6d. per week.

The overhead charges for the sidecar machine are therefore—

	£	s.	d.
Depreciation	25	4	2
Insurance	6	2	0
Tax	4	0	0
Licence		5	0
Garage	6	10	0
	£42	1	2 per annum.

We come now to running costs. These are entirely dependent upon the mileage covered and upon luck. The latter element makes it difficult to forecast the running costs accurately, since new tyres may be badly cut by broken glass, etc., whilst repairs on one machine may be heavier than those on another. The estimates here quoted assume, therefore, average good luck, since allowance for all contingencies would make it impossible to arrive at any standard of running costs whatever.

Petrol and Oil Consumption. Petrol consumption for ordinary mileages is one of the smaller of motor-cycling costs, now that petrol is sold at so low a figure. The price of petrol is constantly fluctuating, but it is assumed to average out at 1s. 4d. a gallon. With careful driving, the solo machine should do 80 miles to the gallon and the sidecar 60 miles. Oil consumption will probably work out at about 4,000 miles per gallon either solo or sidecar, oil being considered to average a cost of 7s. per gallon.

The next important item of running costs is the tyre bill. Provided that the tyres are sufficiently inflated, it is fair to estimate the mileages obtainable with a sidecar to be as follows: rear tyre, 5,000 miles ; front tyre 8,000 miles ; sidecar tyre, indefinite, say, 20,000 miles. On a solo machine it is probable that the rear tyre will do 6,000 miles and the front tyre 10,000.

In calculating running costs it is essential to estimate some mileage per annum ; the examples given hereafter, therefore, are based on (1) 5,000 miles per annum, and (2) 10,000 miles per annum.

Petrol consumption for the solo machine has been estimated

FIG. 16. ARIEL MACHINES FAR FROM THE BEATEN TRACK

at 80 miles per gallon ; so for 5,000 miles, reckoning petrol at 1s. 4d. per gallon, the cost will be approximately £4 3s. 4d. Similarly, the cost for the sidecar machine will be £5 11s. 1d., the 10,000 mile figures being £8 6s. 8d. and £11 2s. 2d. respectively. Oil will cost 8s. 9d. for either type of machine, this being doubled for the 10,000 miles. Five shillings' worth of grease will last an indefinite time ; it is therefore included as a first charge and can be ignored later.

These items complete the running costs, with the exception of repairs and replacements. Tyres, for 5,000, do not enter into the matter, and since the machine is new no replacements or repairs of a major nature should be necessary. It is advisable, however, to set aside a lump sum for minor repairs, and for these £3 should be ample for 5,000 miles ; repairs might be somewhat higher for the 10,000 miles (but not double), and for this purpose £4 10s. is included in the schedule of costs. It is assumed that the rider will decarbonize the engine himself; if he does not intend to do so, the amount charged by the local garage must be ascertained and added.

Running costs for 5,000 miles, therefore, for the solo machine may be estimated to be—

	£	s.	d.
Petrol	4	3	4
Oil		8	9
Grease		5	0
Repairs	3	0	0
	£7	17	1

For the sidecar machines the costs will be—

	£	s.	d
Petrol	5	11	1
Oil		8	9
Grease		5	0
Repairs	3	0	0
	£9	4	10

The Question of Tyres. On the 10,000 mile basis, tyres also have to be taken into consideration. It has been assumed, in the case of the solo machine, that the lives of the rear and front tyres are 6,000 and 10,000 miles respectively. Therefore a new back tyre will have to be bought during the year, and will be two-thirds worn out at the end of the twelve months' running. The tube should not be worn out but, for safety, its price is included in the total of £1 15s., which at the time of writing is the cost of a 26 in. by 3·25 in. Dunlop wired-on cover and tube.

The calculations for the sidecar tyres are carried out in the same way. There must be a new rear tyre—and this will want replacing at the end of the year; there must also be a new front tyre which will, however, be only a quarter worn.

The running costs for the 10,000 mileage are therefore as follows—

SOLO MACHINE

	£	s.	d.
Petrol	8	6	8
Oil		17	6
Grease		5	0
Repairs	4	10	0
Proportion of tyre cost	1	3	4
	£15	2	6

SIDECAR MACHINE

	£	s	d.
Petrol	11	2	2
Oil		17	6
Grease		5	0
Repairs	4	10	0
Proportion of tyre cost	2	3	9
	£18	18	5

RUNNING COSTS OF AN ARIEL MOTOR-CYCLE

To discover the total cost of owning an Ariel motor-cycle it is only necessary to add the overheads to the running costs. The figures work out as follows—

SOLO MACHINE

	5,000 Miles £ s. d.	10,000 Miles £ s. d.
Overhead charges	28 19 2	28 19 2
Running costs	7 17 1	15 2 6
Total	£36 16 3	£44 1 8

SIDECAR MACHINE

	5,000 Miles £ s. d.	10,000 Miles £ s. d.
Overhead charges	42 1 2	42 1 2
Running costs	9 4 10	18 18 5
Total	£51 6 0	£60 19 7

Many riders consider that when they have bought a machine the money spent is gone, and they do not think it worth while to take depreciation into account. Without reckoning depreciation, therefore, the total cost comes out as follows—

	5,000 Miles £ s. d.	10,000 Miles £ s. d.
Solo	17 2 1	24 7 6
Sidecar	26 1 10	35 15 5

The cost per week, which is what interests most riders, is thus, to nearest pennies, 6s. 6d. and 9s. 4d. respectively for the solo machine, and 10s. and 13s. 9d. respectively for the sidecar.

From the figures given above the intending purchaser of an Ariel machine will be able to see at a glance how much motor-cycling is likely to cost him. Should he decide to buy the machine on the easy payment system, he should write to the Ariel Company for particulars of their extended payments system, and by a simple calculation he can gather the probable amount of his weekly or monthly expenditure. It must be borne in mind that the greater the mileage the less will be the total cost per mile.

CHAPTER III

THE LAW, LICENCES, INSURANCE

BEFORE the owner can take a new motor-cycle on the road there are several formalities which must be completed in accordance with existing laws. The first is that the rider himself must have a driving licence. This can be obtained either by personal application or by post from the Town Council of the County Borough in which the owner resides, or from the County Council should he live outside a County Borough. The charge is 5s. per annum, from the date on which the licence is taken out.

A driving licence is the same price whether it entitles the owner to drive a motor-cycle alone or a motor-cycle and a car. The earliest age one can obtain a licence is sixteen, and this applies only to motor-cycles, seventeen years being the youngest at which one can obtain a licence to drive a car also. When applying for a licence, therefore, the prospective motor-cyclist should, if he be seventeen years of age or over, apply for one to cover the driving of both a car and a motor-cycle, since this costs no more and may be useful in the future. A declaration of physical fitness must be made at the time of application. Should a licence be lost or destroyed an application must be made to the local authorities, who are authorized to supply a new one upon payment of 1s.

Renewing a Driving Licence. Although a driving licence is so easy to obtain and costs so little it is one of the motor-cyclist's most valuable possessions for, should he fall foul of the police, it may be suspended for a period. The licence is non-transferable, and the authorities do not give information when its renewal becomes due. The rider must, therefore, make sure that he does not let the twelve months overrun, since he may at any time be pulled up, and, if the licence has expired, will become liable to certain penalties.

After a conviction of a motoring offence the licence may be endorsed on the back, the endorsement carrying particulars of the offence and the penalty inflicted. A police officer, when examining a rider's licence, is not allowed to take note of the endorsements on the back. This is so that he shall not be influenced by any past offences. In a police court itself, too, no reference must be made to endorsements until the magistrates have decided whether the defendant is guilty or otherwise. If they decide the former they may then request the defendant to produce his licence,

THE LAW, LICENCES, INSURANCE   25

so that they may consider his past history before inflicting the fine or other penalties.

The Motor-cyclist and the Police. A few words here may well be said concerning the rider's dealings with the police. The average British policeman is an excellent fellow, polite, and courteous. He is, however, only human, and many riders cause themselves a lot of unnecessary trouble by being rude to him when he stops them. There are very few policemen who want to cause trouble on their own account, but if they are abused it is only natural that they should become annoyed and should exercise their powers to the fullest extent—an extent which may be unpleasant for the rider.

Never try to bribe a policeman. This is a most serious offence, and will probably be met by a very much larger fine than would the original alleged offence for which the rider was stopped.

NEW MOTOR LAWS

The following data has been extracted from the Road Traffic Act, 1930, and it is hoped that this information will be of value to readers of this book.

Accidents (What to do). Stop immediately. Give name and address and registration number of vehicle, if requested. Failing this, the accident must be reported within 24 hours at a police station or to a police constable.

The Minister of Transport may direct an inquiry to be made into the cause of any accident involving a motor vehicle. A person authorized by the Minister may inspect the vehicle, and at a reasonable time enter premises where the vehicle is situated. Obstruction of that person is an offence. The report of an inquiry shall not be used in legal proceedings instituted in consequence of the accident.

Address. If a motorist is alleged to have driven recklessly, dangerously, or carelessly, he must give his name and address to any person having reasonable ground for requiring the information. If he refuses, or gives a false name and address, he is guilty of an offence.

Careless Driving. A person shall not drive without due care and attention or without reasonable consideration for other road users. A first or second conviction for this offence does not entail disqualification for holding or obtaining a licence.

Dangerous Driving. A person shall not drive recklessly, or at a speed or in a manner dangerous to the public.

Penalties—

Not exceeding £50, or up to four months' imprisonment for the first offence.

Not exceeding £100, or up to four months' imprisonment, or to both such fine and imprisonment for the second or subsequent offence.

Six months' imprisonment or a fine (amount unlimited), or to both such imprisonment and fine on conviction or indictment. All convictions to be endorsed on the driving licence, with power to disqualify for holding or obtaining a licence.

Drunkenness. Any person convicted of driving, or attempting to drive, or in charge of a motor vehicle on a road or other public place, when under the influence of drink or drugs to such an extent as to be incapable of having proper control of the vehicle, shall be liable—

(*a*) On summary conviction, to a fine not exceeding £50 or imprisonment up to four months. For a second or subsequent conviction, to a fine not exceeding £100 or up to four months' imprisonment, or to both such fine and imprisonment.

(*b*) On conviction on indictment, to imprisonment up to six months, or to a fine (unlimited) or to both imprisonment and fine.

A police constable may arrest, without warrant, any person committing this offence.

Unless, for special reasons, the Court thinks otherwise, disqualification for a period of twelve months shall follow a conviction. Particulars of conviction and disqualification shall be endorsed on the driving licence.

Eyesight Test. Are you able to read at a distance of 25 yd. in good daylight (with glasses, if worn) a motor-car number plate containing six letters and figures. Applicants who answer " No " to this question are debarred from obtaining a licence.

Horn. A motor vehicle must be fitted with a suitable instrument for giving audible warning of approach where necessary. When a vehicle is stationary on the highway, no person shall use or permit the horn to be used, except when such use is necessary on the grounds of safety.

Lights. Motor-cycles with sidecars attached must show two white lights forward (indicating total width), and a red light showing to the rear.

THE LAW, LICENCES, INSURANCE

Solo machines must carry one white light in front and a red light at the rear, together with proper illumination of the rear number plate (Fig. 18).

Number Plates. Both in the registration book and on the licence card will be found the index letters and number which have been allotted to the machine, and these must be affixed to the number

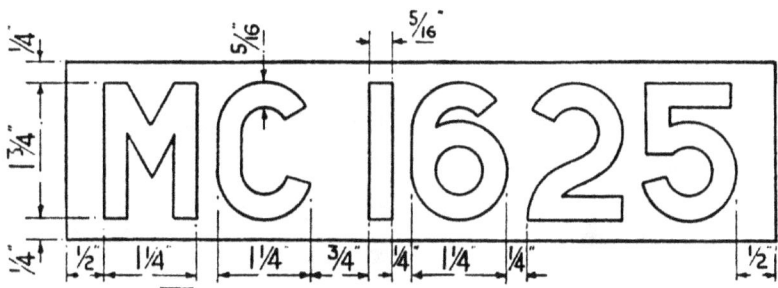

FIG. 17. FRONT NUMBER PLATE DIMENSIONS

plates, the lettering being of the dimensions shown in Figs. 17 and 18.

Insurance. A person may not use or permit any other person to use a motor vehicle on the road unless such use is covered by insurance against third party claims. This does not require the owner to cover a person in his employ against death or bodily injury arising out of and in the course of his employment—a liability which is covered by other statutes.

Where compensation is paid under the provision of compulsory insurance, and where to the knowledge of the insurer a third party has received hospital treatment, the insurer shall also pay to the hospital a sum not exceeding £25 for each person so treated. This obligation does not apply where a charge has already been made by the hospital.

In addition to the usual policy, or cover note, the insurance company shall hand to the owner a "certificate of insurance" in the prescribed form, and when applying for his motor-cycle licence, the applicant must—by production of the insurance certificate or otherwise—satisfy the Licensing Authority that the necessary cover against third party risks will be in force at the time the motor-cycle licence becomes operative.

The driver of a motor vehicle shall, when requested by a police constable, give his name and address, and produce the insurance certificate. If he cannot produce it immediately, he must produce it *in person* within five days at any police station he may specify.

Where an accident occurs involving personal injury to another person, if the driver is unable to produce his certificate at the time, he shall report the accident to a police station as soon as possible, *and in any case within* 24 *hours of the accident*, and shall there produce his certificate. If the certificate is not available for immediate production, the driver may produce it *in person* within five days at any police station he may specify.

Proceedings for offences may be brought (*a*) within six months of the commission of the alleged offence, or (*b*) within a period

Fig. 18. Rear Number Plate Dimensions

which does not exceed three months from the date on which the offence came to the knowledge of the prosecutor, or one year from the date of the commission of the alleged offence, whichever period is the longer.

Penalties—

Up to £50 or imprisonment up to three months, or both such fine and imprisonment. A person convicted under this section is automatically disqualified from holding or obtaining a driving licence for twelve months, but without prejudice to the power of the Court where there are special reasons to order otherwise.

The rider is well advised to insure with a company of good standing. Some small insurance companies may offer policies which show a slight reduction in cost, but as often as not this reduction is far more than outweighed by the difficulty of obtaining satisfactory settlement of claims. The details given below are quoted from the R.A.C. unlimited motor-cycle insurance policy, which is reserved for the exclusive benefit of members and associate members of the Royal Automobile Club. The benefits obtained in the R.A.C. unlimited policy are as follows—

1. CLAIMS BY THE PUBLIC. A full, complete, and unlimited indemnity (excluding passengers) to the insured against all claims made for personal injuries or damage to property or animals by, through, or in connection with the insured motor-cycle or any motor-cycle not belonging to him, provided his own is not in use. Law costs incurred with the Society's consent paid in addition to compensation awarded.

2. FIRE. Loss of or damage to motor-cycle, including sidecar whilst attached thereto, and accessories and spare parts in, on, or about the motor-cycle (whether cycle damaged at the same time or not) by fire, lightning, explosion, or self-ignition.

3. BURGLARY. Loss of or damage to motor-cycle, including sidecar whilst attached thereto, and accessories and spare parts in, on, or about the motor-cycle (if cycle stolen at the same time) by burglary, house-breaking, larceny, or theft, or any attempt thereat.

4. TRANSIT. Loss of or damage to motor-cycle, and sidecar whilst attached thereto, and accessories and spare parts on the cycle during transit by road, rail, or inland waterway in the United Kingdom, and during sea transit between any ports in the United Kingdom or by short sea routes between the United Kingdom, and continent of Europe. A special policy is needed to cover long overseas journeys.

5. ACCIDENTAL OR MALICIOUS DAMAGE to motor-cycle including sidecar whilst attached thereto and accessories and spare parts (whether machine damaged at the same time or not), and the reasonable cost of removing the cycle from the scene of the accident to the nearest competent repairers and their fair charge for re-delivery to the assured. Tyres are also covered if the machine is damaged at the same time.

If no claim is made or arises during any year of insurance, a bonus of 10 per cent of the premium is allowed, provided that the policy is renewed in full. There are also a number of discounts of which the rider may take advantage, just as there are several special charges for exceptional risks.

The discounts are offered if the insured bears various amounts of each claim. If, for instance, he bears the first 50s. there is a 15 per cent reduction, if the first £5, a 20 per cent reduction, if the first £10, a $33\frac{1}{3}$ per cent reduction. These are very substantial, and if the rider feels that he can risk a certain amount of money, he may well take advantage of one or other of them.

Raised Premiums for Pillion Riding. Amongst the additional risks which are covered at an extra price, the most important is that which applies to pillion riding on a solo machine, 50 per cent extra being charged. It must be remembered that, even with the full premiums payable, the machine is only insured for one driver, and the following charges are made for other drivers: one named driver in addition to the insured, 33⅓ per cent extra; any additional driver, 50 per cent extra. A premium of 30s. is charged to cover personal accidents on a certain set basis.

There are a number of special features which are attached to the R.A.C. policy, these being clearly detailed on the proposal form. This policy, or that issued by any first-class company, is recommended to motor-cyclists, and from the details given above it will be seen that third party claims, at any rate, can be covered for a trivial sum.

CHAPTER IV

RUNNING-IN AND DRIVING HINTS

BEFORE setting out on a new machine the first thing to do, obviously, is to fill the oil and petrol tanks. The oil advised by the manufacturers is Castrol XL or XXL, and the fuel recommended is No. 1 petrol for the side-valve models and ordinary benzol mixture for the overhead valve machines. The oil tank should not be filled above the level of the return pipe in the case of the lightweights, or above 1 in. below the return pipe for the medium-weights, and the level should not be allowed to drop below about two-thirds. This leaves a minimum quantity of one pint in circulation. The more oil there is in the tank, the cooler and cleaner it keeps.

Any Ariel model is quite easy to start by means of the kick-starter, provided that the rider sets the levers, etc., in a suitable position and acquires the knack of using the kick-starter efficiently.

When starting for the first time on a solo motor-cycle it will usually be advisable to place the machine on the stand. The petrol should be turned on and the carburettor flooded by two or three sharp depressions of the tickler. The throttle control should therefore only be opened about one-eighth of its movement, the air lever should be closed, and the spark lever set one-third advanced.

Kick-starting. Having carried out these operations, see that the gear lever is in neutral position, and push down the kick-starter pedal until the compression of the engine is felt. Then allow the starter pedal to return to its original position. Lift the exhaust valve lever (not fitted on the 4F) and with the instep of the foot (most riders prefer using the right foot) on the kick-starter pedal, push down the starter as far as it will go, releasing the exhaust valve lever just before the half-way in the travel of the starter pedal; the engine should then fire.

It may, however, back-fire. This shows that everything is in order except that the ignition lever is advanced slightly too far. Retard the ignition lever a little and repeat the operation. As soon as the engine fires, advance the ignition fully and open the air. The speed of the engine should then be adjusted by means of the twist grip throttle control.

On models SB and SG a decompressor is fitted to facilitate starting.

The Oil Supply. On old type Ariels it was then necessary to adjust the regulating screw to the sight feed lubricator, setting it so that it allowed 15 to 20 drops of oil to pass per minute.

Until the rider becomes accustomed to the machine, it is here necessary for him to make absolutely sure that a gear is not engaged. When the machine is on the stand it will, of course, start almost as easily with a gear engaged as with it in the neutral position, and when the engine fires the back wheel will revolve.

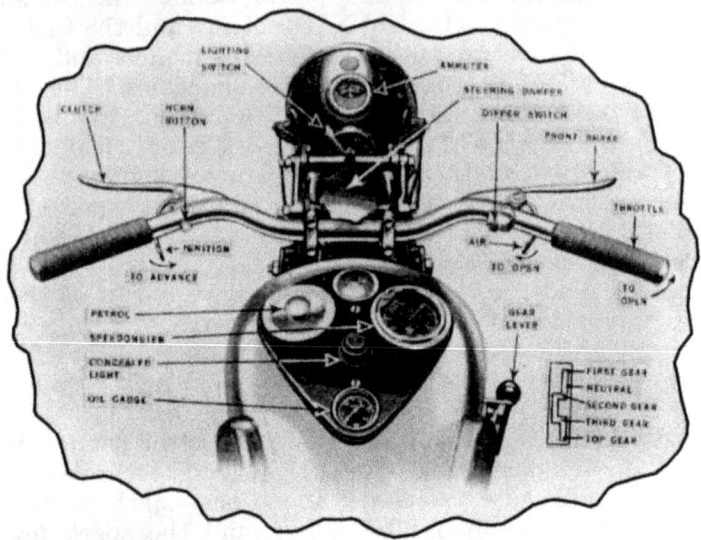

Fig. 19. Showing the Controls of the Ariel Square Four

To make certain, therefore, that the lever has not inadvertently been put in the wrong place, apply the back brake and see that the wheel comes to a stop before pushing the machine off the stand, which will spring up out of the way. Then straddle the machine, keeping both feet on the ground. If the machine is equipped with a steering damper, make sure that this is slacked right off for the first ride; otherwise at a low speed steering will be difficult.

Moving Off. Depress the clutch lever fully and engage first gear. Open the throttle gradually, at the same time letting the clutch in steadily. The machine will then move forward until, at a speed of about 4 miles per hour, the clutch can be fully engaged. It is not advisable for the novice to take his first run on either an uphill or downhill gradient. On the former he may tend to stop his engine by engaging the clutch too rapidly or not giving sufficient throttle opening, and on the latter the machine may tend to run away with him. When a speed of about 8 miles per hour has been obtained, second—or middle—gear should be engaged. To do this close the throttle slightly, lift the clutch, and move the gear smartly into the middle position; then re-engage the clutch and open the throttle.

When the machine has reached a speed of about 20 miles per hour the rider may change into top gear, following the same directions as those which applied to the second gear. When it comes to changing down the method is similar, except that it is not necessary to close the throttle whilst moving the gear lever, although the clutch must, of course, be disengaged. It is not advisable to run on top gear up any gradient at under 20 miles per hour, nor is it wise to change down into second gear at speeds of over 25 miles per hour, and bottom gear at over 10 miles per hour.

Use of the Clutch and Front Brake. It must be remembered that if the clutch is of the cork insert type (although extremely smooth and in every way satisfactory), it should not be slipped unduly. It must not, for instance, be slipped in order to assist the engine up hills. The gear box is made to be used, and in the learning stages gears should be changed frequently, as this will assist the rider in the manipulation of his machine and will also save the engine and clutch.

It should also be borne in mind that the front brake is extremely powerful. It is perfectly smooth and safe in action, but should not be applied harshly. It is advisable, indeed, for the novice to get thoroughly conversant with its action first, so that it can be correctly used when the occasion arises. As a general rule it should be applied gently and slightly after the rear brake. A little practice in this respect will soon give the rider confidence, and once he has obtained this confidence he will find the powerful front brake extremely useful.

The Use of the Steering Damper. When 500 miles have been covered the rider may give his machine full throttle and see how it behaves at speed. Ariel motor-cycles are noted for their excellent steering qualities, but even so the roughness of most roads makes it advisable to use the steering dampers which are fitted to all but the lightweight models. The rider should work up to the feel of speed gradually. As he reaches high speeds, so he should tighten the steering damper slightly, remembering, before slowing down to a single figure speed, to release the damper; otherwise steering will be stiff at these low speeds and he may have considerable difficulty in negotiating sharp corners, etc. On a sidecar machine, incidentally, since the element of balance does not enter into the matter, the steering damper may be kept reasonably tight for all speeds. A little practice in the use of this device will soon make its operation apparent.

Hand Signals. One of the most common causes of accidents is the failure of one or all parties concerned to give the proper hand signals, or to give them at the proper time. Last-minute hand wagging is futile and most dangerous. All signals which are intended to convey anything should be clear, and should be given at a time when the following driver is in a position to heed the warning without having to resort to heavy braking. The signals that should be used are those shown in Fig. 20, and are the ones generally recognized. Implicit reliance should not be placed on the other man paying regard to the signal; the eyes and ears should be used also. When turning right or left into another road, a glance to the rear is the safest policy, as to be rammed broadside is the most dangerous type of mishap possible. If you have a pillion passenger, he, or she, should give the necessary signals to following traffic.

Skidding. Skidding is one of the greatest mishaps that the motor cyclist has to guard against, particularly in unfavourable weather. Below are given a few hints on how to avoid a skid—

(*a*) Interchange the rear with the front cover, or fit a new tyre when the tread wears off the back tyre.

(*b*) Cross tramlines at a wide angle.

(*c*) Apply the brakes gently, the rear one first, and do not declutch.

(*d*) Stop at home if you feel "nervy."

The correction of a front wheel skid is a matter which cannot be fully explained in print, for it is an art which only practice teaches. It is not intended, of course, that readers should deliberately practise front wheel skids, but circumstances so much affect this type of mishap that it is impossible to lay down hard and fast rules concerning it.

To correct a rear wheel skid, steer into the skid and bring the machine under control again if there is room. The important thing is to remain quite calm and to avoid sudden braking.

Subsidiary Roads. Quite a number of accidents occur through a driver entering a main road from a subsidiary road without being aware of the fact, and it is not reasonable to expect main-road traffic to give way, although at present the law concedes no priority to main-road traffic. To prevent this type of accident, the N.S.F.A. have advised, and the suggestion has been adopted,

FIG. 20.—RECOGNIZED SIGNALS TO BE USED BY DRIVERS

A = Signal to stop
B = Slowing down
C = Turning to right
D = Turning to left
E = You may overtake me

that a special sign (shown at *B*, Fig. 21) be erected at dangerous crossings where subsidiary roads are entering main roads, so that drivers need be under no illusion as to the nature of the road upon which they are travelling. The subsidiary road sign (a triangle within a circle) is placed some little distance before the actual danger point, but, of course, only a limited number of roads can be dealt with in this manner.

Danger Signs. Apart from the recently-introduced subsidiary road sign, there are numerous others scattered at various points

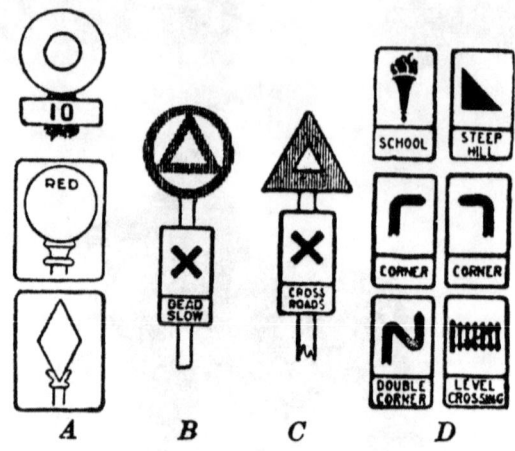

FIG. 21. SOME IMPORTANT ROAD SIGNS

throughout the country. The more important types are shown at *A*, *C*, *D* (Fig. 21). The signs illustrated at *A*, from top to bottom, are, respectively, the local speed limit sign, one indicating that road traffic is prohibited, and a general motor notice. At *C* and *D* are a number of self-explanatary signs indicating crossroads, schools, etc. Local speed limits are in force at numerous places and must be observed.

White Lines. Always faithfully observe the white lines at road intersections and corners. They have already done a vast amount of good and have given a certain sense of security to careful drivers.

Automatic Traffic Indicators. By the end of 1929 automatic traffic control signals almost entirely of the three-light pattern (see Fig. 22) were employed at some fifty centres, and they are now coming into general use.

Red by itself means " Stop " before reaching intersection.

Amber following the red, or simultaneously, means " Prepare to start."

RUNNING-IN AND DRIVING HINTS

Amber following the green means "Stop before reaching the intersection," unless, when the amber first appears, a vehicle is so close to the intersection that it cannot be safely pulled up, in which case it should proceed and get clear of the crossing.

Green means "Go ahead."

At night the showing of the red and green lights is sometimes discontinued, and the amber light only shown, either steady or flashing.

A standard preliminary warning sign has been recommended by the Ministry of Transport to notify drivers that they are approaching such signals, but in many cases no warnings except a "Slow" notice are given. The standard warning sign is also shown at Fig. 22.

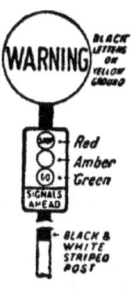

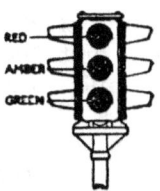

Fig. 22. Automatic Signal (below) and Warning (above)

General Hints. In the following paragraphs a number of hints and tips are given, under the heading of what constitutes bad riding, which are worthy of mention—

1. Racing the engine unnecessarily and letting the clutch in so quickly that the wheel skids or jerks the machine forward. *Take a pride in a neat getaway.*

2. Jamming on the brakes at the last minute instead of slowing down steadily. *Drive on the throttle and not the brakes.*

3. Racing the engine or grinding the gears when changing gear. *A good driver is a neat driver.*

4. Applying the brakes when rounding corners instead of slowing down before reaching them. *Brake early and be neater, safer, and faster.*

5. Remaining in top gear when the engine is obviously labouring, instead of dropping down into a lower gear. *Never force an unwilling engine.*

6. Opening the throttle quickly when the machine is travelling slowly, thus causing the engine to "pink." *Change down for a quick "getaway."*

7. Running with the ignition too far retarded, causing overheating and loss of power. *Advance the ignition as far as the engine will allow.*

8. Using the exhaust lifter lever to slow down instead of shutting the throttle. *The exhaust lifter is for starting only.*

9. Holding the clutch "out" too long instead of dropping into neutral. *Excessive slipping soon heats up the clutch.*

10. Interfering with the silencing system to obtain a heavy bark. *Silence is fine, but noise brings a fine.*

11. Using the machine when out of adjustment. *Check everything over at frequent intervals.*

12. Taking unnecessary risks. *Obey the rules of the road scrupulously.*

The instructions applying to the novice's first ride have been given briefly only, but it is hoped that they are sufficient to indicate the method of procedure. We will now discuss the very important matter of running-in the engine.

Running-in. Every Ariel machine is fitted with an aluminium piston. Now for the best results to be obtained from an aluminium piston, as well as from the engine generally, it is essential that the first few hundred miles should be run at a moderate speed.

Some manufacturers instruct riders of their machines that a speed of 20 to 25 miles per hour should not be exceeded during the first 500 miles. Actually the makers of the Ariel say that 30 miles per hour should not be exceeded for the first 400 or 500 miles. This is as much as can be said in any brief warning, but it is far more important that the engine should not be allowed to labour than it is that it should be kept below definite speeds. For the engine to give good results later in its life, it is important that throughout the running-in period of, say, 500 miles, the throttle opening should never be very great, and that the actual internal heat should be kept as low as possible. Descending a slight hill on half throttle at, say, 40 miles per hour, will do far less harm than climbing the same hill on full throttle at 25 miles per hour. Similarly, the ascent of a steep hill on a sidecar machine using second gear may be very injurious to a new engine if a wide throttle opening be needed, even if the speed of the machine be only 10 to 15 miles per hour. *Light running*, therefore, is what must be aimed at during the first 500 miles. Towards the end of this distance it will do no harm to open the throttle for occasional short spells, but it must not be kept open for any length of time ; violent acceleration should be avoided.

It is extremely difficult, especially for the accomplished rider, to refrain from opening out during the earlier periods, but abstinence in this respect is well worth while. He can console himself, moreover, with the knowledge that expert track and road-racing motor-cyclists pay particular attention to this matter unless, of course, they know that the engine has already been run-in for many hours on the bench. This is possible in the case of specially made racing engines, but would make the price of production models prohibitive.

CHAPTER V

THE FOUR-STROKE ENGINE

SINCE it is probable that over 90 per cent of the readers of this book are fully familiar with the working of the internal combustion engine, the briefest details of it only will be given in these pages. For those who do not know " the front from the back " an encyclopaedia is recommended ; experts should skip the following elementary chapter.

Motor-cycle engines are of two types—two-stroke and four-stroke. All Ariel engines are of the latter type, which is so known since the piston makes four distinct movements, or strokes, for each power impulse. The main components of a single-cylinder, four-stroke, motor-cycle engine are: cylinder, valves, piston, connecting rod, flywheels, little- and big-ends, main shaft, cam gear, and crankcase.

The cylinder is no more than a " pot," by which name, incidentally, it is often known, and in it the piston moves up and down. A gudgeon pin passes through the walls of the piston (strengthened by bosses) and the little-end of the connecting rod. The big-end of the connecting rod is attached to the flywheels by a crank pin, and from the centre of each flywheel protrudes a short, stiff main shaft ; these shafts are free to revolve in bearings in the crankcase. The near-side shaft extends through the crankcase and has a driving sprocket attached to it ; the offside shaft operates the cam gear.

The Working Operations. A reference to Fig. 23 will make it clear that as the flywheels revolve so the piston must move up and down ; the amount of its movement is known as the engine's " stroke." At the top of the cylinder are two valves—an inlet and an exhaust. Fresh gas from the carburettor is drawn into the cylinder via the inlet valve and expelled, when burnt, through the exhaust valve. In order that the valves should open and close when desired, cams are fitted in the crankcase. These cams are driven by the main shaft and lift each valve once every alternate revolution. Springs are attached to the valves in order to return them to the seatings, and to make the upper part of the cylinder—the combustion chamber—gas tight. The piston has slots cut in it to receive spring rings, known as piston rings. These prevent gas from blowing past the walls of the piston and yet allow the latter to have a sufficient working clearance.

Imagine the piston at its uppermost position—at the top of its "stroke." The four "strokes" are then as follows—

INLET. The inlet valve opens and the piston descends. A partial

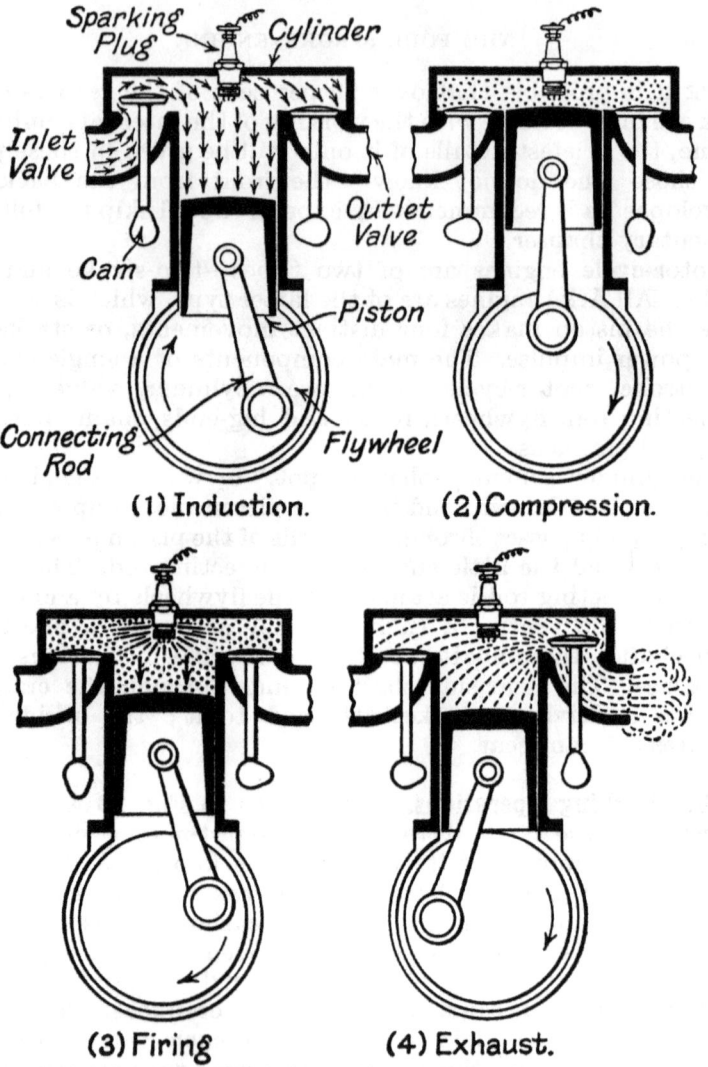

FIG. 23. THE PRINCIPLE OF THE FOUR-STROKE ENGINE

vacuum draws gas from the carburettor into the combustion chamber. The piston reaches the bottom of its stroke and reverses.

COMPRESSION. The inlet valve closes as the piston rises. Nothing else opens at the top, so the gas becomes compressed.

THE FOUR-STROKE ENGINE

COMBUSTION. When the piston has reached the top of its stroke and has thus finished compressing the gases, a spark appears at the points of the sparking plug and ignites the gases. This combustion, which is the only power impulse of the four strokes, drives the piston downwards.

EXHAUST. Just before the piston reaches the bottom of its combustion stroke the exhaust valve opens and the piston, rising, pushes the burnt gases out of the cylinder. At approximately the top of the stroke the exhaust valve closes, the inlet valve opens, and the cycle of operations is repeated.

That, briefly, is the action of the four-stroke engine. It must also be mentioned that the carburettor is a device for mixing liquid petrol with air and allowing controlled amounts of the mixture to enter the combustion chamber; the electric current for the sparks is also supplied by an instrument known as a magneto, which is driven from an extension of the cam wheel.

On Ariel engines the various parts are made of the following materials: cylinder, cast iron; valves, steel; piston, aluminium; connecting rod, steel; flywheels, cast iron; big-end, main shafts, and cam gear, steel; crankcase, aluminium.

Location of Valve Gear. The valves are disposed in two ways. On the " LB 32," " MB 32," " VB 32," and " SB 32 " models they are set side by side, with their heads in the side of the combustion chamber and their stems pointing downwards; an engine with this valve disposition is known as a side-valve engine. On the " LF 32," " MF 32," " VG 32," " VH 32," and " 4F 32 " models the valve heads are in the top of the cylinder and their stems point upwards, these engines being therefore called overhead valve engines. The orifice through which the gas enters is called the inlet port; that through which it is expelled is called the exhaust port.

Side-valve Ariel engines have one of each ports, the single cylinder overhead valve engines having one inlet and two exhaust ports, with the exception of model MF 32, which has a single exhaust port.

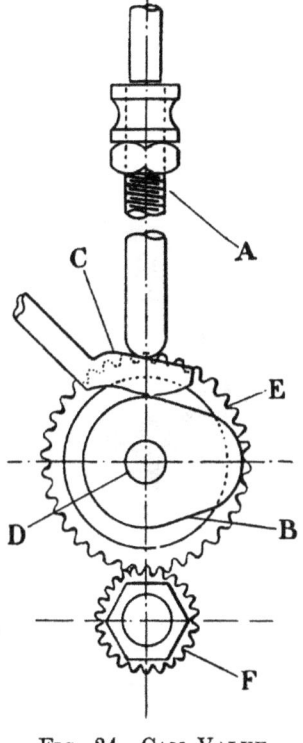

FIG. 24. CAM VALVE ACTION

THE PRINCIPLE OF THE CARBURETTOR

It has been found by experiment that the most satisfactory way of encouraging petrol to evaporate is to drive it under pressure through a very tiny hole, called a jet, and the process is assisted by heating the spraying device. Owing to the proximity of the carburettor to the combustion chamber, ample heat is, of course, conducted to it *via* the induction pipe, once the engine has warmed

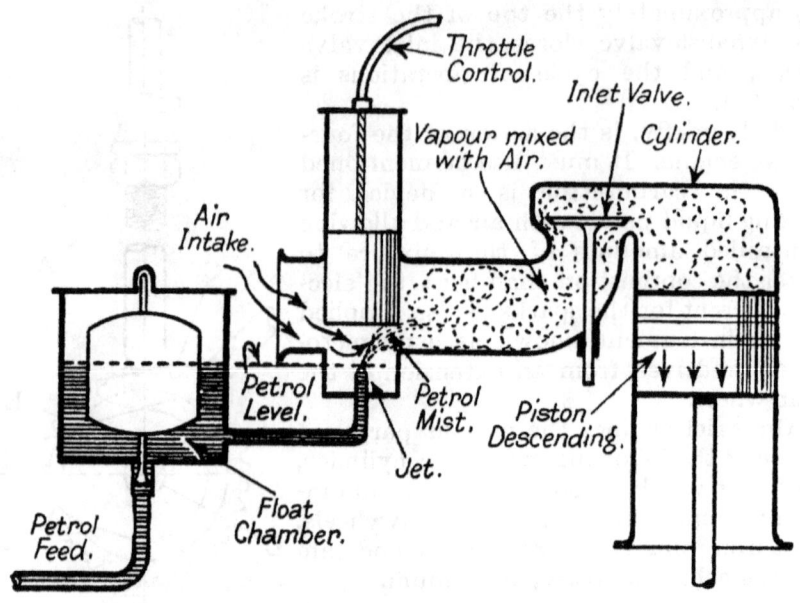

FIG. 25. ILLUSTRATING PRINCIPLE OF THE CARBURETTOR

up. The powerful suction through the inlet pipe on the inlet stroke can be relied upon to atomize the fuel completely. Let us refer to Fig. 25, which shows the salient features of a carburettor in action. It will be observed that the petrol level in the jet must be below the orifice at the top; otherwise the petrol will overflow and cause *flooding* of the carburettor. The level is automatically regulated by the action of a *float* attached to a spindle, which operates a needle valve, thereby cutting off the petrol supply immediately the level in the chamber reaches the height of the jet orifice. On the downward stroke of the piston, air is sucked in through the air intake; past the partially open throttle, which is a closely fitting hand-controlled slide, operating up and down in a barrel; past the jet; past the inlet valve, and thence into the cylinder. The extremely high velocity air current that must obviously sweep over the jet causes the fuel to issue in a small fountain, and simultaneously causes the spirit to be atomized and diffused with the air rushing in towards the combustion chamber. This, briefly, is the principle of the carburettor.

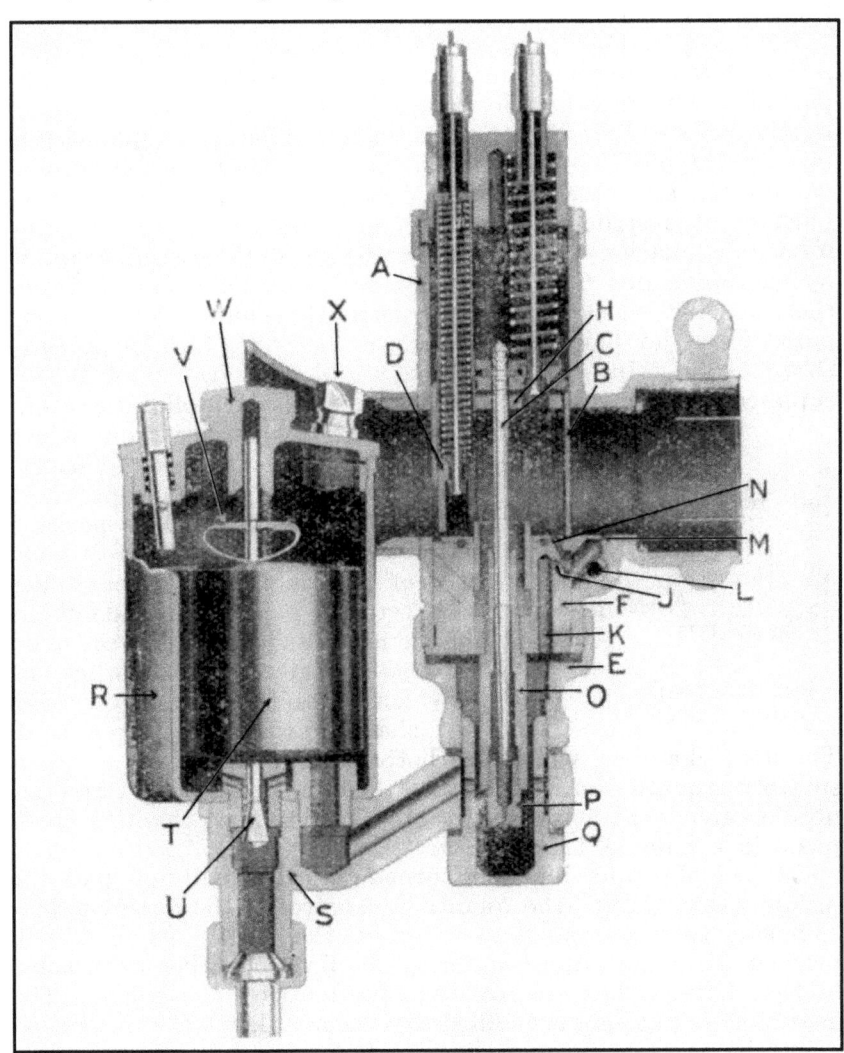

Fig. 26. Sectional View of Two-lever Variable Jet Amal Carburettor

The various refinements and complications that are incorporated in the Amal carburettor are designed to (1) make the mixture as homogeneous as possible; (2) simplify the control; (3) enable automatic slow running to be obtained; (4) enable settings for special purposes to be made.

THE AMAL CARBURETTOR

This carburettor incorporates all the best features of B. & B., Binks, and Amac types. The following description will enable the reader to comprehend its working.

Referring to Fig. 26, showing a sectional view of the instrument, A is the carburettor body or mixing chamber, the upper part of which has a throttle valve B, with taper needle C attached by the needle clip. The throttle valve regulates the quantity of mixture supplied to the engine. Passing through the throttle valve is the air valve D, independently operated, and serving the purpose of obstructing the main air passage for starting and mixture regulation. Fixed to the underside of the mixing chamber by the union nut E is the jet block F, and interposed between them is a fibre washer to ensure a petrol-tight joint. On the upper part of the jet block is the adaptor body H, forming a clean through-way. Integral with the jet block is the pilot jet J, supplied through the passage K. The adjustable pilot air intake L communicates with a chamber, from which issues the pilot outlet M and the by-pass N. An adjusting screw (TS, Fig. 27) is provided at the mixing chamber, by which the position of the throttle valve for tick-over is regulated independently of the cable adjustment. The needle jet O is screwed in the underside of the jet block and carries at its bottom end the main jet P. Both these jets are removable when the jet plug Q, which bolts the mixing chamber and the float chamber together, is removed.

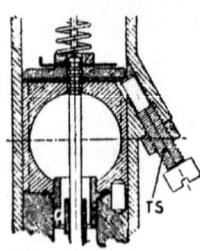

FIG. 27. AMAL THROTTLE STOP

The float chamber, which has bottom feed, consists of a cup R suitably mounted on a platform S containing a float T, and the needle valve U attached by the clip V. The float chamber cover has a lock screw X for security.

The petrol tap having been turned on, petrol will flow past the needle valve U until the quantity of petrol in the chamber R is sufficient to raise the float T, when the needle valve U will prevent a further supply entering the float chamber until some in the chamber has already been used up by the engine. The float chamber having been filled to its correct level, the fuel passes along the passages through diagonal holes in the jet plug Q, when it will be in communication with the main jet P and the pilot feed hole K; the level in these jets being, obviously, the same as that maintained in the float chamber.

Imagine the throttle valve B very slightly open. As the piston descends, a partial vacuum is created in the carburettor, causing a rush of air through the pilot air hole L, and drawing fuel from the pilot jet J. The mixture of air and fuel is admitted to the

THE FOUR-STROKE ENGINE

engine, through the pilot outlet M. The quantity of mixture capable of being passed by the pilot outlet M is insufficient to run the engine. This mixture also carries excess of fuel. Consequently, before a combustible mixture is admitted, throttle valve B must be slightly raised, admitting a further supply of air from the main air intake. The farther the throttle valve is opened the less will be the depression on the outlet M, but, in turn, a higher depression will be created on the by-pass N, and the pilot mixture will flow from this passage as well as from the outlet M.

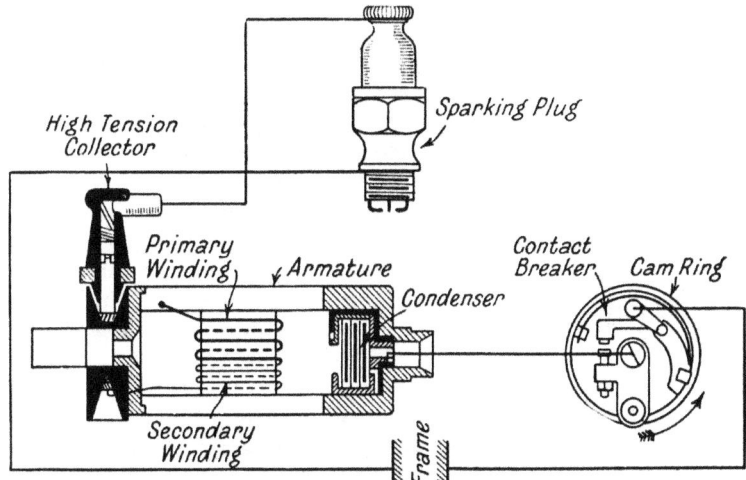

FIG. 28. MAGNETO IGNITION WIRING DIAGRAM

As the throttle valve is farther opened the fuel passes the main jet P, which governs the mixture strength from seven-eighths to full throttle. For intermediate throttle positions the taper needle C, working in the needle jet O, is the governing factor. The farther the throttle valve is lifted the greater the quantity of air admitted to the engine, and a suitable graduation of fuel supply is maintained by means of the taper needle. The air valve D, which is cable operated on the two-lever carburettor, has the effect of obstructing the main through-way, and, in consequence, increasing on the depression the main jet, enriching the mixture.

THE PRINCIPLE OF THE MAGNETO

The magneto primarily consists of three parts: (1) the *armature*; (2) a *U-shaped magnet*; (3) the *contact breaker*.

The armature comprises an iron core or bobbin of " H " section, on which are two windings; firstly, a short winding of fairly heavy gauge wire; and, secondly, on top of the former, a very big winding of fine wire. The first winding is known as the *primary* and the second as the *secondary* (see Fig. 28). The armature, which can rotate on ball bearings, is placed such that on rotation it periodically cuts across the *magnetic field* of the magnet, and creates a current in the primary winding. Incidentally, the contact breaker forms part of the primary circuit. This current, however, is at a very low voltage—far and away too small to produce anything in the nature of a spark. But if a *break* is suddenly caused in the primary by separating the platinum contacts when the current is at its maximum flow, a high voltage or tension current will be instantly *induced* in the secondary winding —sufficient to jump a small space, if the circuit be incomplete. In this circuit the sparking plug is included, and things are so arranged that, in order for the secondary circuit to be complete, the current must jump across the electrodes of the plug, or, in other words, a spark must occur. Now in the case of a single cylinder engine, the points in the rotating contact breaker separate once in every armature revolution (there being one cam only), and the armature to which the contact breaker is fitted being driven off the exhaust camshaft by sprockets and chain runs at half-engine speed; that is to say, a " break " takes place once every two engine revolutions, i.e. four strokes of the piston. Hence, if the initial " break " be timed to occur when the piston is at the top of the compression stroke, all the other " breaks " (and therefore sparks) will occur at this point also, and thus the engine will go on firing correctly. Besides the " break " being timed to take place when the piston is in a certain position (which we call " timing the magneto," see page 81), it must also be timed to occur at the moment when the bobbin is having the greatest effect on the magnetic field (see Fig. 29). This, of course, is allowed for in the design of the magneto, and does not really concern the reader. Also, it is essential that the primary circuit should be complete (i.e. the contacts must be properly closed) both before and after the " break," which should be of very short duration.

FIG. 29. POSITION OF MAGNETO ARMATURE WHEN CONTACTS SHOULD OPEN

The *cam ring*, against which the cam of the contact breaker works, can be rotated by handlebar control through about 15°, thereby giving means of advancing and retarding the spark.

The *condenser* is a device for the purpose of eliminating "arcing," and the *pick-up* is a small carbon brush kept in continual contact with the *slip-ring*, in order to collect or pick up the H.T. current for the sparking plug lead.

CHAPTER VI

MAINTENANCE AND OVERHAULING

IN this chapter the author has aimed at putting in a convenient form all that information and data necessary to enable the Ariel owner to keep his machine and engine in first-class trim, and this it is hoped will be of value both to novices and experts. All motor-cycles, and for that matter all mechanical contrivances, require periodic lubrication, minor adjustments, and occasional overhauling; at regular intervals the I.C. engine requires to be decarbonized and the valves ground-in if a reasonable degree of efficiency is to be maintained.

The accessibility and straightforward design of the Ariel makes adjustments and overhauling a very simple matter, and decarbonization is by no means a tedious proposition if the rider gets to work in a methodical manner and uses the right tools for the job.

There are a number of minor adjustments which it is desirable that the Ariel rider should attend to every few hundred miles, or when circumstances necessitate these adjustments being made. If the rider values his machine, however, he will not wait until adjustment *has* to be made, but will carefully inspect his machine as a matter of routine and make the necessary adjustments before they become essential. By doing this, much time and money is in the long run saved, and the performance of the machine will be kept at its maximum.

ROUTINE ADJUSTMENTS

Cleaning. It requires a considerable amount of time to keep a motor-cycle in anything approaching "showroom" condition, but it is the author's opinion that, unless a machine is kept reasonably clean, the fullest pleasure and maximum efficiency cannot be obtained from it. Apart from the question of pride of ownership, it is an undoubted fact that dirt covers a multitude of defects and greatly accelerates depreciation in respect of market value. This is, of course, obvious. If neglected, a motor-cycle rapidly becomes shabby and an eyesore. After a ride in dirty weather, cleaning may take at least an hour. It entails the use of stiff bristle brushes and paraffin for removing the filth from the lower extremities, together with cloths, leather, and polish for the enamelled parts. On no account should a machine be left wet overnight, or a serious amount of rusting may ensue. If the rider is so busy that he cannot spare the time for cleaning, the machine should be thoroughly greased all over before use.

It should be noted that chromium plating does not require and should not be treated with metal polish, for it does not oxidize in the same manner as nickel-plating. The chromium-plated parts should be treated similarly to the enamel, and the surfaces will then improve with cleaning.

Periodical Inspection of Nuts. One of the most important points in connection with the care of a motor-cycle is to look over

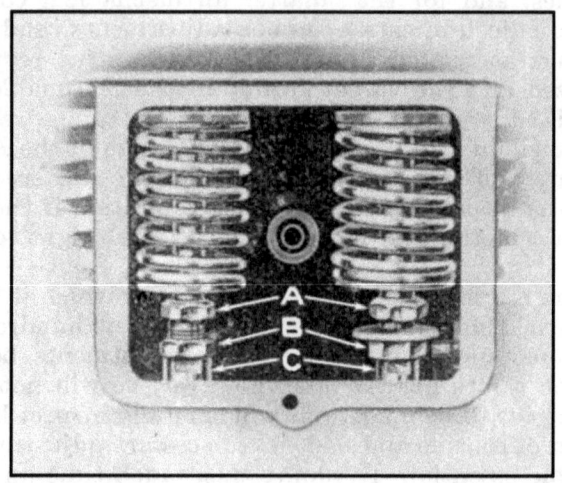

FIG. 30. ADJUSTING TAPPETS (S.V. ENGINE)

the machine frequently and apply a spanner to any nuts which have worked at all loose.

Tappet Adjustment. When the engine has been rebuilt it will probably be found that the tappets require adjustment, and the procedure is as follows—

S.V. and Lightweight O.H.V. Models. Remove the valve spring or tappet spring cover and set the engine with the piston somewhere near the top of the cylinder with both valves fully closed. To adjust the tappets, the tappet C (Fig. 30) should be held while the lock nut B is loosened. Then rotate A, holding the tappet C until the desired clearance is obtained. Now secure the lock nut B and recheck the clearance several times whilst rotating the engine from the position where the inlet valve closes until the exhaust valve opens.

MAINTENANCE AND OVERHAULING 49

On the S.V. engine the clearance is measured between the top of the tappet head and the end of the valve stem. Do not be confused by there being no clearance for a few degrees just after the inlet valve closes and just before the exhaust valve opens: this is quite correct.

On the 4-valve models the clearance must be checked between the adjuster on the end of the rocker arm and the hardened steel cap on the end of the valve stem. A most practical way of checking the adjustment is to make sure the clearance is practically nil by seeing that it is impossible to depress the end of the rocker arm, and then testing for compression. If this is satisfactory, it is clear that the valves are seating correctly. If there is no compression, either a valve is being held off its seat through too close adjustment, or there is a serious leakage elsewhere. In either case the cause must be found and rectified.

O.H.C. Model. The adjustment on this model is extremely simple and is carried out as follows—

Remove the cover from the rocker-box, and unclip the distributor from the end of the rocker-box. Regard the back plate, on to which the distributor cover fits, as a clock face. Rotate the engine until the insulated centre piece on the end of the camshaft is pointing to half-past seven. Both valves of No. 1 cylinder are now closed and adjustment can be carried out. Slack off the lock nut X (Fig. 31) and rotate the adjuster Y until the desired clearance is obtained; then holding Y lock up X dead tight. Similarly adjust the clearance for the inlet valve. The clearance is easily measured between the valve stem end-cap and the end of the adjuster screw. Now rotate the engine a little more until the centre piece Z (Fig. 38) points to half-past four. Adjust the valve clearances of No. 2 cylinder. The valve clearances of Nos. 3 and 4 cylinders are adjusted in a similar manner.

The correct clearances with the engine cold are as follows—

Model	Inlet (in.)	Exhaust (in.)
S.V.	·002	·004
O.H.V.	Nil	Nil
O.H.C.	·002	·002

Exhaust Valve-lifter Adjustment. It is important that there should not be an entire absence of backlash at the exhaust valve-lifter lever with the exhaust valve fully closed, which would inevitably prevent the exhaust valve from seating properly, and thus cause loss of compression and burning of the valve and its seating, accompanied probably by intermittent banging in the exhaust pipe and silencer. There should be about $\frac{1}{16}$ in. backlash at the handlebar control, and the desired adjustment may be

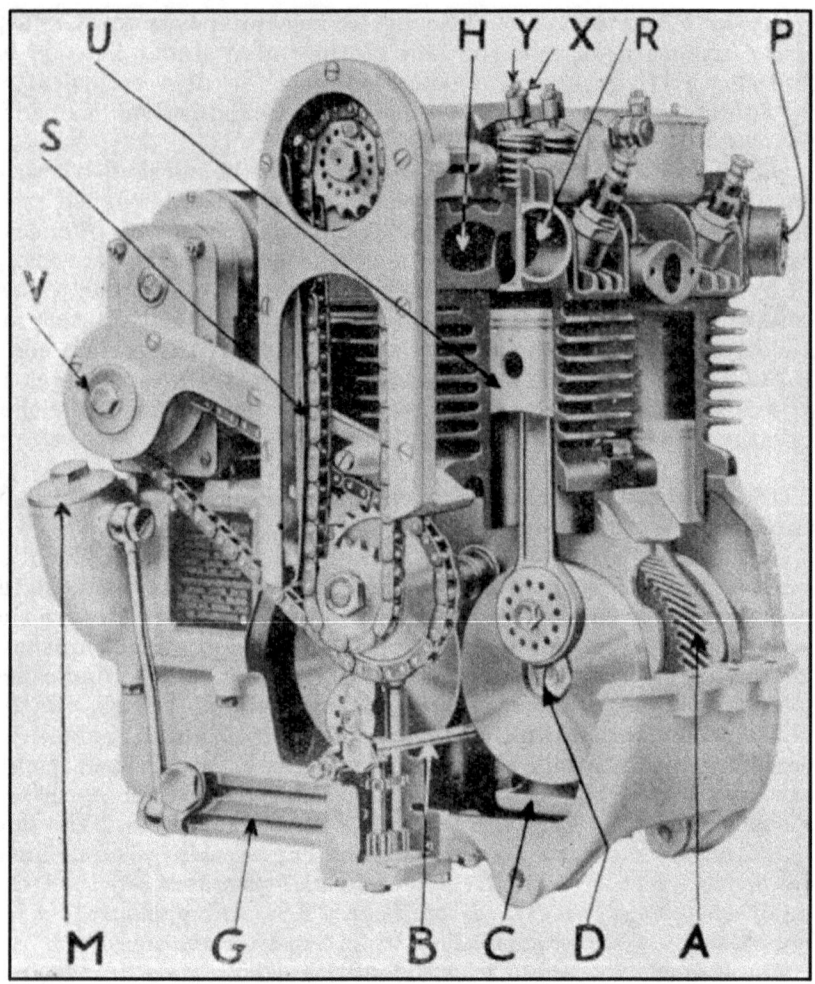

Fig. 31. Front Side View of Sectioned Engine
(4F Model)

This view shows the general design of the engine and particularly the front crank arrangement, oil pump, and camshaft drive.

KEY TO FIG. 31

A = Main crankshaft gears
B = Oil delivery tube to centre gearcase
C = Oil trough for connecting rod dipper D
D = Dipper on connecting rod, for splash lubrication
G = Return oilway from engine sump to oil reservoir
H = Exhaust gas passage from No. 2 cylinder to port R
M = Oil reservoir filler cap
P = Exhaust port for Nos. 3 and 4 cylinders
R = Exhaust port for Nos. 1 and 2 cylinders
S = Automatic spring tensioning device for camshaft chain
U = Slot for gudgeon pin circlip removal
V = Inspection plug for magneto sprocket and fixing

made by loosening the lock-nut on the cable adjuster stop and screwing the adjuster in or out as required a few turns. After adjusting re-tighten the locknut.

A further means of adjustment is to alter the setting of the exhaust lifter arm on the eccentric spindle. This is only held by a nut and taper. To slack off the taper joint, undo the nut a couple of turns, and give the face of the nut a light sharp blow, so as to drive the eccentric spindle inwards. Set the arm as required and tighten up the nut securely.

The Sparking Plug. Difficult starting or occasional misfiring can usually be traced to a dirty or defective sparking plug. The life of a Lodge plug is considerable, but the points of the electrodes gradually burn away and eventually the gap becomes enlarged considerably, and it is necessary to reset the points with the aid of a feeler gauge. The correct gap is ·02 in. (i.e. about twice the contact-breaker gap). Excessive gap at the plug points means that the voltage required from the magneto is higher; and this not only renders starting difficult, but—what is worse— causes brush discharge inside the magneto. This discharge eventually causes internal corrosion, and the efficiency of the magneto is impaired. From time to time the plug should be removed and thoroughly cleaned with petrol, both inside and outside. All deposits of soot or charred oil must be eliminated, as these are apt to cause leakage and bad running. The insulation should be examined for cracks or flaws, and in very humid weather should be wiped dry with a rag before starting-up. The accepted method of testing for current at the plug terminal is to place a wooden-handled screw-driver, with steel blade, across the terminal and just touching the cylinder fin, when a spark should be visible on rotating the engine. To test the plug itself, remove it with the H.T. lead still affixed, clean it, lay it on the cylinder, and note whether it sparks satisfactorily when the engine is rotated. If it does not, scrap it. Always fit the correct type of plug recommended by the manufacturers.

The Contact-breaker. The magneto should not be interfered with unnecessarily, for it is a very delicate instrument, and functions best when left well alone; but at regular intervals, say every 1,000 miles, the contact-breaker cover should be removed and the contacts (see Fig. 32) should be examined, and their gap checked with a 12 thou' feeler gauge. If the clearance is excessive, the timing will be advanced and the primary circuit will not be closed for the correct period, and occasional misfiring is very likely. Provided the contacts are kept clean and, above all, *free from oil*, they will probably need adjustment only at long intervals.

It is not desirable to alter the setting unless the gap varies considerably from that of the magneto spanner gauge. If adjustment is necessary, rotate the engine round slowly until the points are seen to be fully opened, and then, using the magneto spanner, slacken the lock-nut and rotate the fixed contact screw by its hexagonal head until the correct gap is obtained, as indicated by the feeler gauge; then screw up the lock-nut firmly.

If, when the contact points are examined, it is found that they have become burned or blackened (owing probably to the presence

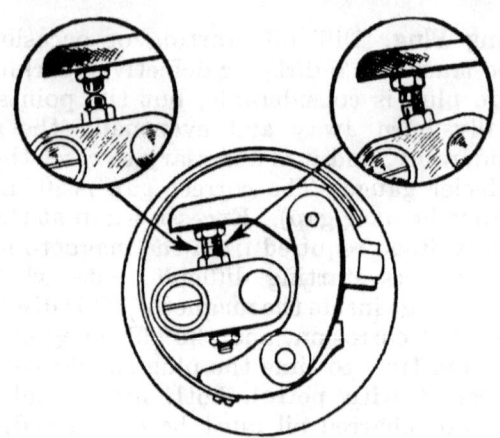

(From " The Motor Cycle ")
Fig. 32. The Points should Close as shown in the Bottom Circle and Not as Above

at some time or other of dirt or oil), they may be cleaned with very fine emery cloth, and afterwards with a cloth damped with petrol. All dirt and metal dust must be wiped away entirely. Where the contacts are found to have become seriously pitted, it may be advisable to go over the surfaces with a dead smooth file and only the very smallest amount of metal should be removed. Removing the contact-breaker unit will assist filing the contacts quite true, which is imperative.

Any sign of incipient rusting on the contact-breaker spring should be checked immediately, as rust and corrosion are frequent causes of broken contact-breaker springs.

In the case of the M-L contact-breaker, it is as well occasionally to examine the plunger and control spring, and to grease these thoroughly, as any rusting here may possibly cause binding of the control and sticking of the tappet in its guide.

The Primary Chain. Since this is automatically lubricated and totally enclosed, stretching takes considerably longer than is the case with the secondary chain, which is much more exposed

MAINTENANCE AND OVERHAULING

to harmful influences. However, it will stretch in time, and it must be retensioned correctly. If a chain is too slack, it is apt to "whip," which intensifies the wear and tends to break the rollers, especially in the case of the front chain. On the other hand, if it be too tight, a crushing stress is produced on the rollers, and the whole chain is subjected to unfair stresses, and the sprockets wear quickly. The chain should be adjusted and kept adjusted, so that it can be given midway by pressure with the fingers a total and maximum deflection of $\frac{3}{8}$ in. Adjustment is effected by slackening the four sleeve nuts retaining the gear-box to the bottom bracket, and by means of the drawbolt pulling the box rearwards gradually until the correct tension is arrived at. After making an adjustment, see that the gear control has not been upset.

The Secondary Chain. The secondary chain requires to be tensioned at regular intervals, depending upon the mileage of the machine and how the rider has lubricated the chain. This chain should undergo a total maximum deflection of $\frac{3}{4}$ in. when properly adjusted. To do this, loosen the rear wheel axle nuts and screw up the two special drawbolts in the fork ends, afterwards re-tightening up all nuts firmly. See that wheel alignment is not put out when tightening the drawbolts, and also that the brake operation is not affected. Make whatever further adjustments are found necessary. A rough-and-ready method of testing a chain for wear is to hold a length between the hands and observe to what extent the chain will bend sideways.

Front Forks. A new type of fork adjustment was introduced for 1932 and it is now possible easily to take up wear in the links, as well as to set the friction discs which are provided to damp out oscillations.

To make an adjustment of the spindles, slacken the two hexagon lock nuts, one at each end of the spindle, and re-tighten the spindle by means of a spanner placed on the squared nut. An anti-clockwise rotation tightens the links. It should be noted that re-tightening the lock nut, which is not squared, will tighten up the adjustment, therefore adjust a little at a time, screw up the lock nut, and test. If the adjustment is not right, it is necessary to repeat the process until the correct adjustment is reached.

The reason that the tightening up of the lock nut effects the adjustment is that the spindle at this end is stepped, the shoulder bearing up against a corresponding shoulder in the hole through the link. When the lock nut is loosened, the link moves away from the shoulder on the spindle and extra clearance therefore develops. For correct spindle adjustment the forks should move freely with the dampers out of action, and with no side play on the links.

To bring the fork dampers into action, adjust the spindle which passes through the damper discs, as already described, then loosen the lock nut, give the spindle a partial turn in an anti-clockwise direction and re-tighten the lock nut. If the damping action is then insufficient the spindle has not been rotated far enough. For the best results the forks should have a free action, with just sufficient friction to prevent excessive fork bounce on bad roads. No matter how carefully adjusted, forks will never work properly unless they are kept well greased.

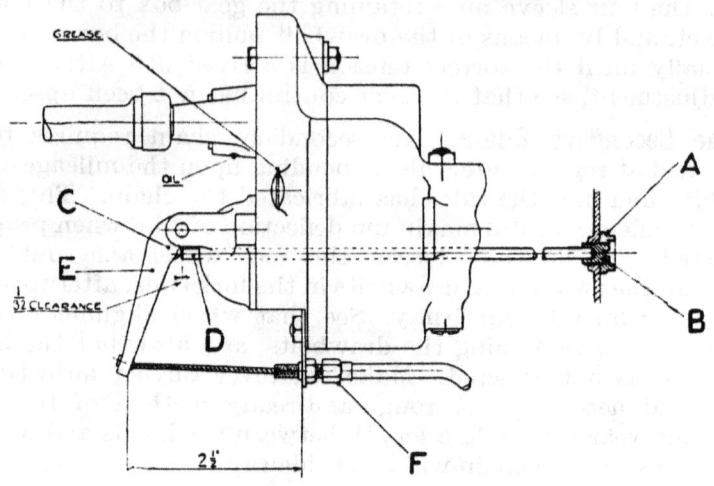

Fig. 33. Clutch Adjustment
(All Three-Speed Gear Boxes)

Clutch Adjustment (Three-Speed Gear Boxes). Adjustment is rarely necessary, and all is correct as long as the spring nuts stand level with the face of the spring plate. After adjusting the clutch, see that the spring plate lifts equally; if not, the nuts should be eased off on the low side and tightened on the high side until it does.

There should always be $\frac{1}{32}$ in. clearance between the ball C in the clutch operating lever E (Fig. 33) and the end of the operating rod D. The end of the operating lever E must be set by means of the cable adjuster F, so that its end is $2\frac{1}{2}$ in. from the outer face of the cable adjuster lug. Then adjust A and B to give the necessary clearance. On the 1931 VF the end of the operating lever E must be set by means of the cable adjuster F, so that its end is $2\frac{1}{2}$ in. *below the bottom* face of the cable adjuster lug. Adjust A and B as above. This setting gives equal movement of the operating lever on each side of the centre line of its pivot with a minimum of wear on the wire cable.

MAINTENANCE AND OVERHAULING

To adjust the clutch on models SB, SG, and 4F, see that there is always a thirty-second of an inch clearance between the ball C in the clutch operating lever E (see Figs. 34 and 35) and the end of the operating rod D. The end of the operating lever E must be set by means of the cable adjuster F so that its end is approximately 3 in. from the face of the cable adjuster lug on the gear-box. This setting gives equal movement of the operating lever on each side of the centre line of its pivot with a minimum of wear on the wire cable. This position of the lever E is obtained by adjusting A and B to give the necessary clearance. To get at these parts it is, of course, necessary to take off the outer half of the primary chain cover, but as the correct setting is given to the lever when the machine is assembled it will rarely be necessary to make this adjustment. In general, maintain a thirty-second clearance between the ball and the operating rod by adjusting the cable adjuster F. (Fig. 34.) When inspecting the clutch at any time, see that the spring nuts stand level with the face of the spring plate, and see that this spring plate lifts equally; if it tends to tilt to one side when lifting, the nuts should be eased off on the low side and tightened on the high side. A tipping plate will tend towards slight clutch drag.

Should oil get on the clutch, as may occur when newly assembled, this will cause slipping; to overcome, inject petrol. A sure sign of slipping is given by the clutch becoming very warm whilst driving.

When fitting up the control wire for the clutch, ease off the bends as much as possible to ensure long life and easy movement of the inner wire, and keep the cable greased where friction occurs.

Steering-head Adjustment. This should be such that it allows perfect freedom without up-and-down play. To test this, stand astride the machine and grip the bars. Lift them to ascertain if any movement is visible. Loosen nut on ball-head clip, then tighten the large column nut. Play in the steering head is liable to damage the ball races, and also causes a tendency for instability on grease, as does play in the wheel bearings.

Handlebar Adjustment. All Ariel machines have handlebars of a type which may be readily adjusted for reach by undoing two nuts. Full advantage should be taken of this to obtain a really comfortable riding position suited to the owner's stature, and there is no need to adopt a "sit-up-and-beg" position nor a road hog crouch. A happy medium should be struck.

All the 1932 Ariels are fitted with "clean" handlebars, the term "clean" being applied to bars on which the controls are integral and not of the clip-on type.

56 THE BOOK OF THE ARIEL

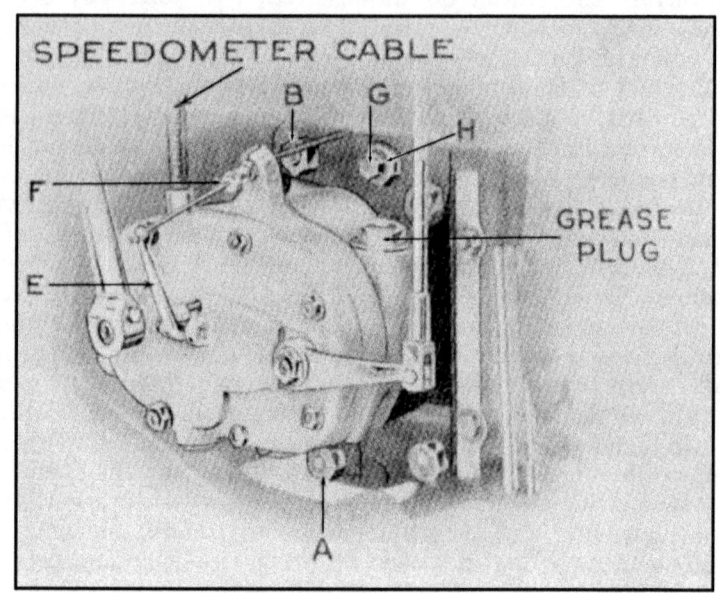

Fig. 34. Clutch Adjustment
(Models SB, SG, 4F)

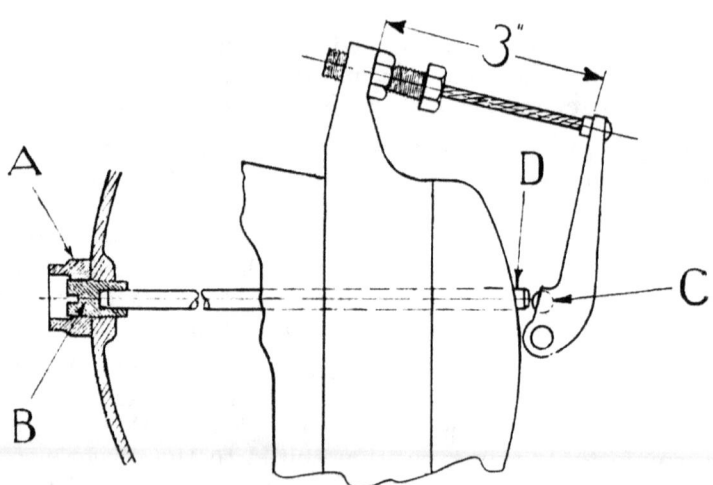

Fig. 35. Clutch Adjustment
(Models SB, SG, 4F)

MAINTENANCE AND OVERHAULING 57

To remove a wire cable from the handlebar, it is first necessary to take out the hexagon-headed bolt and the small cheese-headed set bolt (under bar) which secure the levers and bracket assembly inside the bar. When the levers and bracket have been pulled out of their housing, it is possible to remove and fit the cable in the ordinary manner.

To disconnect the cable from the carburettor or magneto twist-grip, it is first necessary to undo the slotted screw at the end of the grip, which may then be pulled off the bar. Now remove the double coil-spring washer and the plain washers which will be found inside. These may possibly stick, but, if they do, it is quite easy to tap them out ready for replacement.

The operating slide, etc., may now be removed. These parts are contained in a cylinder which fits inside the end of the bar, and which is held in position by means of a peg (integral with the cylinder) located in a guide slot cut in the end of the handlebar. To remove the cylinder: (a) Tap on the end of the flat-sided piece which projects from the end of the bar, until the peg is *forward* in the short slot; (b) rotate the end piece so that the peg moves across into the long slot; (c) pull the end piece *outwards*, so sliding the peg down the long groove.

Now pull out the round-headed pin which is in the wide slot along one side of the cylinder, taking care not to loose the collar, or roller, on the pin. The wire can now be pushed slightly into the body of the cylinder, so releasing the nipple, and then lifted out through the slot. To re-fit, reverse the order given, remembering that the plain packing washers come next to the bar end, with the spring washer outside. Also see that the two flats on the sides of the rotating centre-piece register with the corresponding flats *inside* the end of the rubber grip. Tighten the fixing screw securely.

Wire Controls. Always keep the extremities of the cables well lubricated, and take up slack by means of the adjustable cable stops as soon as it develops. Nothing is more detrimental to the performance of a machine than sluggish or incomplete control action.

Lubrication of Engine. This is by the latest type of lubrication system and combines great economy with the most efficient lubrication.

With this system the lubrication of the engine is entirely automatic, and all the rider has to do is to keep the oil tank replenished and clean out the filters, etc., as required. An oil pressure gauge mounted in the petrol tank indicates a pressure immediately the oil begins to circulate, and so long as the pressure is maintained it shows that oil is circulating correctly. Should the gauge fail, or should the rider feel in any way dubious about the oil circulation, it is easily checked by removing the oil filler cap (with the engine running), and seeing that oil is being returned from the engine to the tank *via* the oil pipe just beneath the filler cap.

To obtain the best results the following grades of oil should be used. Castrol XL for the S.V. models in cool weather, and XXL in hot weather. XXL should be used for all purposes on the O.H.V. models except racing, when Castrol R should be used. On model 4F, the following grades of Castrol should be used: XXL for general use, and R for racing. Never mix Castrol R, which is a vegetable oil, with other oils, or mineral oils such as Castrol XXL.

Furthermore, it should be remembered that when changing over from R to a mineral oil, or *vice versa*, in a four-cylinder engine, it is not sufficient merely to drain the crank case. The whole engine must be dismantled and thoroughly cleaned.

The reason for this is that the oiling system of the four-cylinder engine incorporates a number of troughs and oil ducts from which it is impossible for lubricating oil to escape by itself, even though the sump may be drained.

The Ariel Oil Purifier. The centrifugal oil purifier, which is incorporated in the fly-wheel, is an absolutely automatic and mechanical device for separating dust, grit, dirt, etc., from the oil. No matter how clean an oil is used, dirt and grit will get drawn into the engine *via* the carburettor, and unless this grit is removed immediately it will help to wear away the bearings. The Ariel oil purifier removes this grit as soon as ever it gets into the circulating oil. The action of the oil purifier is as follows—

The oil leaves the hollow timing side mainshaft and passes half-way along the steel tube A (Fig. 36), emerging at the hole B; this tube is solid at the end away from the centre of the fly-wheel. As the oil passes from the tube into the reservoir C, the dirt and grit, etc., is thrown by centrifugal force into the cupped cleaning plug D, whilst the purified oil travels back towards the centre of the fly-wheel and enters the crankpin *via* the passage E.

To get at the purifier, remove the crankcase sump by undoing the four set bolts, and drop the sump complete with filter. Rotate the engine until the plug D is immediately above the sump and then undo the plug; this is locked in position by means of a tab washer. When the plug is removed, the dirt (if present in any quantity) will be found packed quite hard inside the cup formed in the plug, and must be removed with the blade of a penknife. See that the tube A is not damaged, and if it drops out replace with the large end in the plug. The plug locates the tube and keeps it in position.

MAINTENANCE AND OVERHAULING 59

When replacing the plug, see that it is screwed up dead tight *and do not forget the tab washer*; one end must be turned up by the side of a flat on the plug. Use a new tab washer every second or third time the plug is removed, as repeated bending of the metal will cause the end tab to break off the washer.

The sump filter should, of course, be cleaned whilst detached. When replacing, see that the suction pipe is located in the hole in the top of the gauze, and do not forget the joint washer. Wire up the set bolts to prevent loss.

Similar remarks as to cleaning also apply to the filter in the base of the oil tank. Unscrew the hexagon plug at the back of

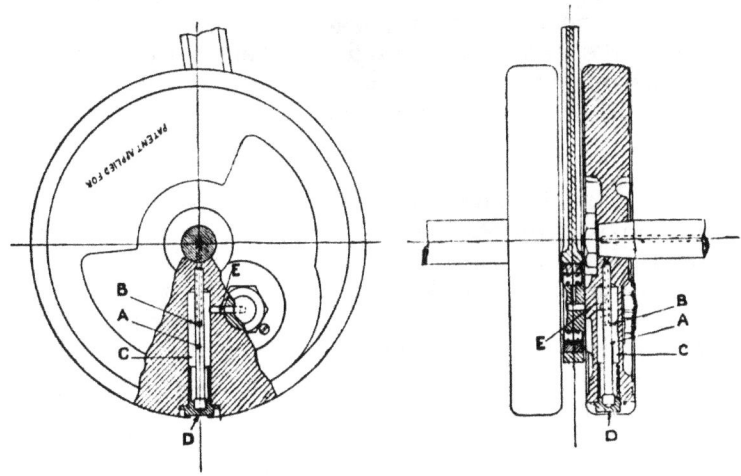

FIG. 36. THE ARIEL OIL PURIFIER

the tank, clean the gauze in petrol and replace. See that the delivery oil pipe, which projects right into the tank in line with the filter, is located inside the gauze and screw up the plug securely.

The dirt which has collected in the cupped plug *D* should be cleared away about every 5,000 to 8,000 miles under normal conditions of use. Where the motor-cycle is used in particularly dusty conditions, so that there is a proportionately greater chance of grit being drawn in through the carburettor, the plug can be removed for cleaning at shorter intervals.

Although the Ariel oil purifier will remove all dirt, etc., from the oil, it cannot turn old oil into new, and it therefore becomes necessary to throw away the used oil as it loses its lubricating properties. This is recommended about every 2,500 miles. A suitable drain plug is provided at the bottom of the oil tank.

Lubrication Chart. Although Fig. 37 shows a model LF 31, it applies in general to the whole range, but is intended as a guide rather than to be scrupulously complied with. In the case of the S.V. models, there is, of course, no rocker-box to lubricate; while on the overhead camshaft machine there is a rocker-box, but it is automatically lubricated.

Lubrication of Gear Box. Second in importance to proper engine lubrication is the correct lubrication of the countershaft gear box, whose function it is to transmit the whole of the engine thrust to the rear wheel.

Once every 1,000 miles, or more often when a large amount of riding is undertaken in very hilly districts necessitating the frequent use of the lower gears, the gear box should be replenished with Wakefield's "Castrolease Medium" through the large screw plug just behind the gear control arm. On no account use gear oils, engine oil, or thicker grease than that recommended above.

DECARBONIZATION

After about 2,000 miles have been covered, the accumulation of carbon deposits on the piston crown and in various parts of the combustion chamber results in the engine losing its original "kick," and there is a marked decline in general all-round performance, accompanied by a tendency to knocking under the slightest provocation. In addition, the exhaust note becomes "woolly." When this happens it is a sure indication that the time has come for undertaking a "top overhaul," or, in other words, for decarbonizing and grinding-in the valves. Carbon deposits are inevitable in internal combustion engines and are due to three things: (a) burnt lubricating oil; (b) carbonization of road dust; (c) incomplete fuel combustion. When decarbonizing it is always worth while inspecting the valve seatings and, *if necessary*, grinding-in the valves. Removal of the valves incidentally facilitates thorough cleaning of the ports.

In connection with decarbonization there are three types of engine to be taken account: (a) the side-valve engine; (b) the overhead-valve engine; (c) the overhead-camshaft engine. The general procedure of decarbonizing is much the same in each case, although structural variations render the operations somewhat different.

Removing the Rocker-box. It is quite unnecessary to dismantle the rocker-box when decarbonizing, but the procedure is as follows—

Models LF, MF, and MH. Undo the three nuts outside one of the plates, when the plate with box and rockers will come away.

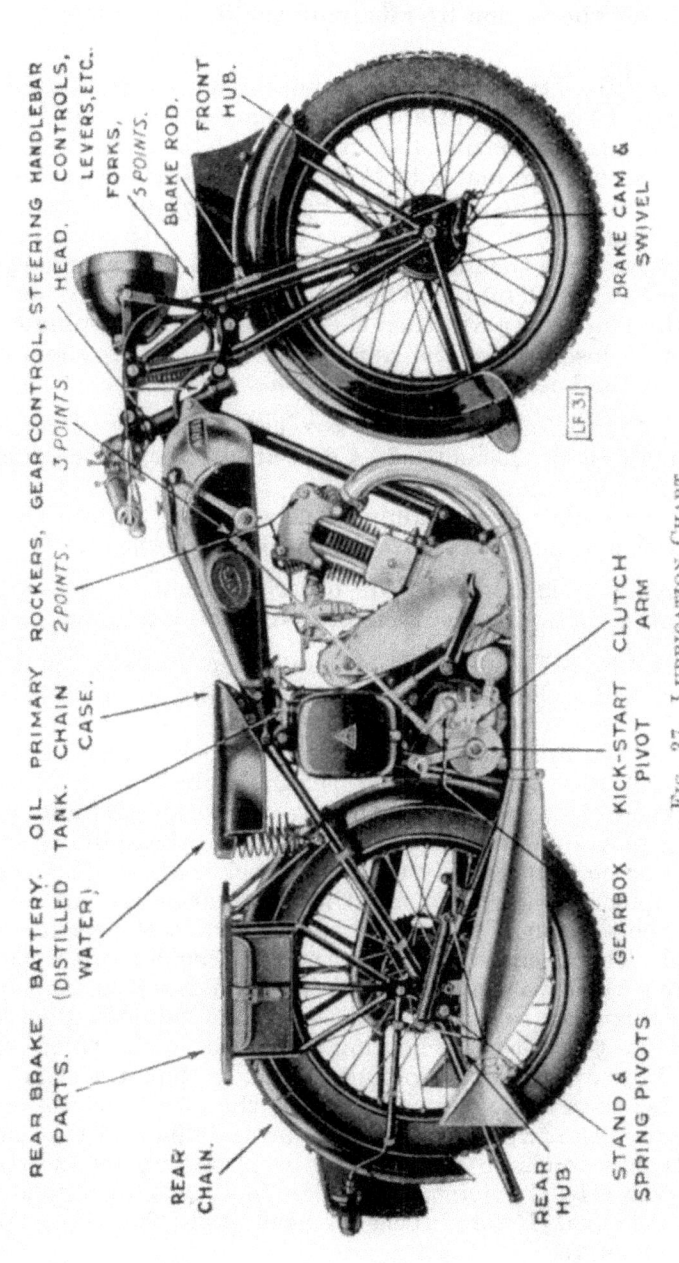

Fig. 37. Lubrication Chart

If desired, the rocker gear can be inspected when the box is in position on the engine by removing the offside supporting plate only.

Models VG, VH, and SG. The box is made in two halves and is fixed to the head by means of side plates. The rocker spindles and nuts form the means of securing the plates to the box, whilst set bolts secure the plates to the head. Undo the rocker spindle nuts and take off the side plates. Split the box by taking out the ten securing screws. Each rocker, complete with spindle, roller bearings, etc., can then be taken out of the box. To dismantle the roller bearings, pull off the flanged collars; this leaves the bearings exposed. The rocker will then slide straight off the spindle; take care not to lose any of the rollers, and note the washers in the rockers at the back of each set of rollers.

Model 4F. Before the rocker-box can be removed the valve gear must first be dismantled as described later, after which the procedure is as follows—

The four rocker box retaining studs T (Fig. 38) are then unscrewed, when the rocker-box will be free of the head.

Removing Cylinder Head. In order to remove the cylinder head on the O.H.V. models, the procedure is as follows—

Models LF, MF, and MH. Remove the sparking plug, carburettor, and exhaust pipes. Set the engine with both valves closed.

Fix the two link plates to support the rocker arms; these are the two plates with projecting pegs, supplied in the tool kit. The method of use is to undo the two rocker spindle nuts on the sparking plug side, and slip the plates on to the spindles so that the pegs come immediately under the rocker arms. Replace and tighten up the spindle nuts, and the rocker arms are held in place against the tension of the return springs, when the rocker-box is removed. This greatly facilitates the replacement of the box.

Remove the two cylinder head bolts on the rear side of the engine; this also releases the rocker plate on this side. Next unscrew the two set bolts holding the offside rocker plate to the head and lift up the rocker-box complete, so that it is clear of the push rods; then draw it away towards the offside of the engine. Now remove the two offside head-securing bolts and take off the head. If this tends to stick it can be prised up by inserting a screwdriver into the joint. Take care not to damage the joint or break the fins. Before lifting the head, undo the oil pipe to the inlet valve guide.

Now remove the valves, when the head and ports can be cleared of carbon and the valves ground in.

MAINTENANCE AND OVERHAULING 63

Models VG and VH. The procedure for removing the cylinder on these models is carried out in a similar way, but on account of

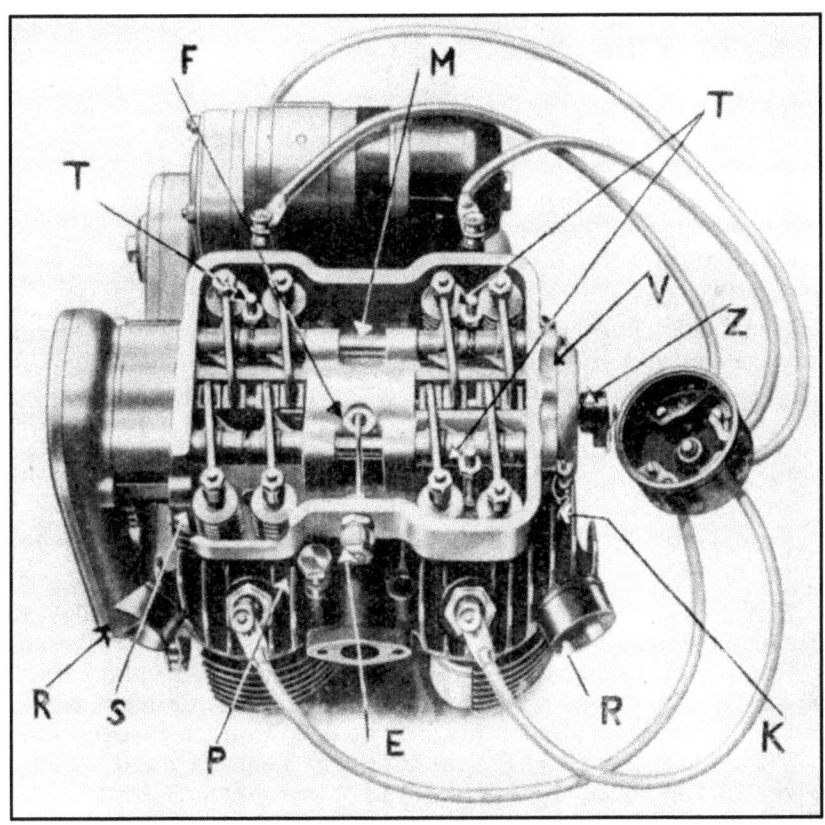

FIG. 38. SHOWING GENERAL ARRANGEMENT OF THE VALVES AND ROCKER GEAR ON THE SQUARE-FOUR

KEY TO FIG. 38

E = Oil delivery union to rocker box
F = Oil delivery hole to camshaft tunnel
K = Spring clip holding distributor cover
M = Rocker lever spindle for Nos. 2 and 3 cylinders
P = Cylinder head securing bolt
R = Exhaust ports
S = Vale spring collar
T = Rocker-box securing studs
V = Distributor cover back plate
Z = Distributor centre piece

differences in construction the following additional notes have been included.

Remove the sparking plug, carburettor, and exhaust pipes. Set the engine so that both valves are closed, release the oil pipe to the inlet valve guides, and unscrew the special hollow set-bolt which forms the connection for the top end of the pipe, and which also helps to secure the rocker box. Now remove the other three set-bolts holding the rocker box to the head; it is desirable to have all valves closed whilst these bolts are being removed. This frees the rocker box, push rods, and enclosing tubes, which can all be removed.

Place a clean rag over the two holes at the top of the timing case into which the push rods fit, so as to prevent the ingress of dirt. Undo the five head retaining bolts. These screw *up* into the head through bosses on the side of the cylinder barrel. Now take off the head, taking care not to damage the joint or break fins.

Model SG. The head (Fig. 39) is removed in a very similar manner, but it will be noted that the rocker-box is held to the head by means of three ordinary set bolts and one special hollow set bolt; this latter carries the upper end of the oil pipe for inlet valve guide lubrication. The head itself is secured by five set bolts screwing *upwards* through bosses on the side of the cylinder barrel.

Now remove the valves, when the head and ports can be cleared of carbon and the valves ground in.

Model 4F. The procedure when preparing this model for decarbonizing is as follows—

Remove the exhaust pipes, sparking plugs, and air and throttle slides from the mixing chamber. The carburettor itself can be left bolted to the cylinder head if the petrol pipe is disconnected.

Push back the two clips K (Fig. 38) securing the distributor cover to the rocker-box, and tie up the cover and leads out of the way.

Unscrew the four thumb nuts securing the rocker-box cover, and lift this off. Take care not to damage the joint washer.

Disconnect the oil pipe to the rocker-box by unscrewing the outer nut on the union E (Fig. 38). The oil restrictor piece on the end of the oil pipe can then be slipped free.

Take off the connection in the pressure pipe to the oil gauge. This connection is just above the rocker-box cover.

Unscrew the plug in the top of the camshaft chaincase. This is similar to the one L (Fig. 40) in the magneto chaincase. This exposes the sprocket securing bolt M; unscrew this bolt and remove. Insert into this hole a flanged collar which is provided in the tool kit. This collar is somewhat similar to the plug which has just been removed, but it has no thread, and has a hole through its centre. Through this hole place the extractor bolt and screw this up into the sprocket. This will pull the sprocket

MAINTENANCE AND OVERHAULING

off the camshaft, and leave the extractor bolt and collar in position. These, and the false bearing in the back of the chaincase, will hold the sprocket and so prevent the valve timing being upset through the camshaft sprocket coming out of mesh with the chain. Do not touch the vernier bolt Z. Remove the two cheese-head screws Q.

Now unscrew the four head-securing nuts. One of these is

Fig. 39. The Four Valve Cylinder Head (Model SG)

This illustration shows the disposition of the four valves. The rocker gear is neatly enclosed in an aluminium alloy casing.

shown at N (Fig. 40). Another nut is just in front of the camshaft chain cover and the other two nuts are in a corresponding position on the other side of the engine. Next remove the four head-retaining bolts, one of which is shown at P (Fig. 38). A similar bolt is on the other side of the induction pipe, whilst the remaining two bolts are in a corresponding position at the back of the engine.

The head is now perfectly free and can be removed by inserting a screwdriver into the joint face between the barrel and the head, and prising up. The joint is made by means of a copper asbestos washer so that care must be taken not to damage this washer with the screwdriver blade. The head must also be lifted straight up to allow the four studs (on which the nuts screw) to come clear of the cylinder block. It will probably be easier to prise up the block simultaneously from two opposite sides. Lift the head clear and place it carefully on the bench, using care with the distributor centre piece as this is easily damaged if knocked.

Fig. 40. Rear Side View of Sectioned Four-Cylinder Engine

KEY TO FIG. 40

- A = Magneto pick-up
- C = Oil trough for connecting rod dipper D (Fig. 34)
- F = Delivery oilway from oil reservoir to engine
- G = Return oilway from engine sump to oil reservoir
- H = Oil regulator: (a) Outer hexagon—adjuster screw
  - (b) Centre hexagon—adjuster screw locknut
  - (c) Inner hexagon—regulator body
- J = Screw plug carrying oil delivery tube B (Fig. 34)
- L = Inspection plug for magneto sprocket and fixing
- M = Camshaft sprocket securing bolt
- N = Cylinder head fixing stud nut
- Q = Cheese-head screws holding camshaft chain case to rocker-box
- V = Camshaft sprocket
- W = Plug carrying oil reservoir filter
- Z = Fixing screw for camshaft vernier arrangement

MAINTENANCE AND OVERHAULING

Removing the Cylinder (S.V. Engines). Remove the sparking plug, valve caps, carburettor, exhaust pipe, and exhaust valve lifter wire.

Now remove the four nuts and spring washers holding down the cylinder, and lift the cylinder up. On the LB engine there are five holding down nuts, one of these being inside the valve spring chamber. As soon as the cylinder is clear of the securing

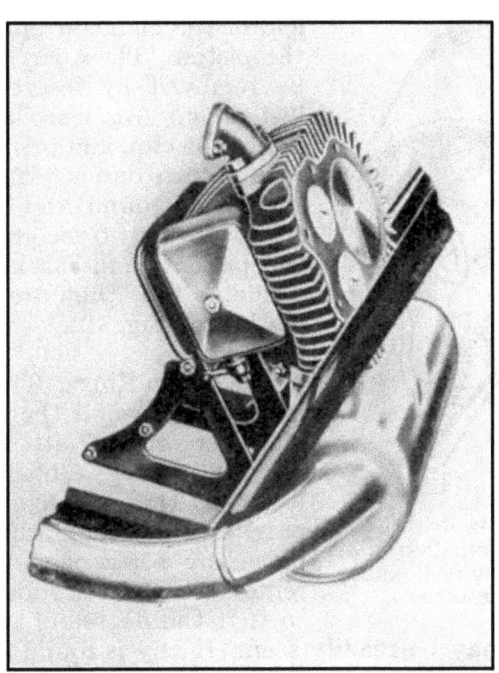

FIG. 41. THE CYLINDER WITH THE
DETACHABLE HEAD REMOVED
(MODEL SB)

studs, incline it forwards and lift up towards the front of the tank. Pull the piston down to the bottom of the stroke and the cylinder will come away.

On engines with detachable heads the procedure is slightly different. Take out the sparking plug, undo the seven set-bolts, securing the cylinder head to the barrel, and lift off the head. Take care not to damage the copper asbestos joint washer.

When complete removal of the cylinder is necessary the procedure is as follows. Undo the carburettor, silencer, and exhaust valve lifter wire; now undo the four-cylinder base retaining nuts and lift the cylinder up and forwards through the two front frame tubes. Push the piston down to the bottom of its stroke and the cylinder will come away. The front wheel should be turned over on to full lock one way or the other to give the necessary clearance for this operation.

Piston Removal. The gudgeon pin is of the fully floating type, i.e. free to rotate in the piston and connecting rod bush. The pin is held in position by means of two spring circlips which fit into grooves machined at each outer end of the gudgeon pin hole through the piston. These circlips can easily be removed by inserting a pointed instrument (e.g. a scriber) in the slot, under the clip, and prising out. Take care not to damage the clip, which should be round and lie flat when removed. On no account interchange the pistons, and mark them on the inside so that they are replaced correctly (see Fig. 42).

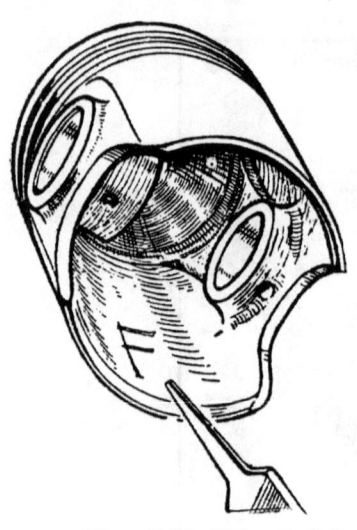

(From " The Motor Cycle")
FIG. 42. MARKING INSIDE OF PISTON TO ENSURE CORRECT REPLACEMENT

The Piston Rings. The rings should be polished round the whole of their diameter, and if either ring is discoloured or has a black patch on it it means that gas has been leaking past, and it should therefore be replaced by a new one. With the rings removed the piston should be washed, so that the degree of carbon deposit in the slots may be readily seen. If any is found here it should be scraped away, but extreme care is necessary in order that the surface of the slot is not damaged by the scraping tool. If it is, loss of compression will result, and if the slot is badly cut or dented a new piston will probably have to be fitted for first-class results to be obtained. Any carbon deposit on the inside of the ring should also be scraped away. It is important to note that the rings should be quite free in their grooves, without much up-and-down movement—the actual amount is ·003 in. when new, and the gap between the ends of the ring should be from ·004 in. to ·006 in. on the 4F, LB, and LF models, and from ·006 in. to ·008 in. on the remaining models.

The word "gap" does not apply here to the distance between the ends of the ring with the cylinder removed; it means the actual gap in working conditions. The only way to test this gap is to push the ring itself into the cylinder bore, making sure that it is square with the walls. The gap may then be measured with

MAINTENANCE AND OVERHAULING

a feeler gauge. If it is less than ·006 in. and ·008 in. respectively, it is advisable to remove a little metal from either one or other end of the ring until the recommended gap is obtained. The reason for this is that should the gap be too small the expansion of the engine, when it becomes hot, will actually cause the ends of the ring to meet, and may make the ring a very tight fit in the cylinder walls, resulting in a loss of power and possibly seizure.

The piston and rings must again be washed in paraffin, after the carbon deposit has been removed. Refitting the rings is quite a simple matter. Before this is done a few drops of oil should be placed in the slots and the top ring may then be pushed over the top of the piston until it is home, the reverse direction applying to the bottom ring.

Removing the Carbon. Thoroughness in decarbonizing well repays the labour expended. The more completely the carbon is removed the better will the engine performance be, and the longer will it be before decarbonizing again becomes necessary. It is inadvisable, however, to decarbonize the piston ring grooves more than about once every 5,000 miles, when the cylinder as well as the cylinder head should be removed. When undertaking an ordinary top overhaul every 2,000 miles, the carbon deposits on the piston crown and on the inside of the cylinder head need alone be scraped off. To do this, a moderately sharp penknife, or the end of a screwdriver, should be employed. Be careful, however, not to employ excessive force on the piston, or its comparatively soft aluminium surface will be deeply scratched. When decarbonizing the cylinder head, do not overlook the exhaust ports, which are usually heavily sooted or carbonized, and, as before mentioned, see that the face on the overhead valve head is not scratched. A good method of holding the head when decarbonizing it is to fit a hexagon steel bar screwed at one end into the sparking plug hole. The cylinder head may then be held in a vice by means of the bar. If a bar is unavailable, an old sparking plug makes a good substitute. After the deposits have been removed, clean the surfaces with a calico rag damped in paraffin.

In the case of the model LB where the entire cylinder has to be removed, the top of the piston may afterwards be rubbed with *very fine* emery cloth until a perfectly smooth surface has been obtained. This method of finishing off may also be used for the detachable heads on all models, but the pistons should not be thus treated except when the cylinder itself is removed, enabling all abrasive particles to be afterwards eradicated. Emery particles which get down on to the rings may cause bad scoring of the cylinder walls. On model LB the deposits on the integral cylinder head may be reached through the cylinder mouth. Care should be taken not to allow the screwdriver shank to scratch the part of the cylinder included in the piston stroke. See also that all carbon is removed from the valve caps, which may afterwards be cleaned with emery cloth.

When occasion is had to remove the piston or pistons, do not attempt to remove carbon from the outside of the skirt. Only the crown, the inside, and the piston ring grooves should be scraped and cleaned. The latter may be cleaned of all deposits after the rings have been removed by running a small, sharp, flat-

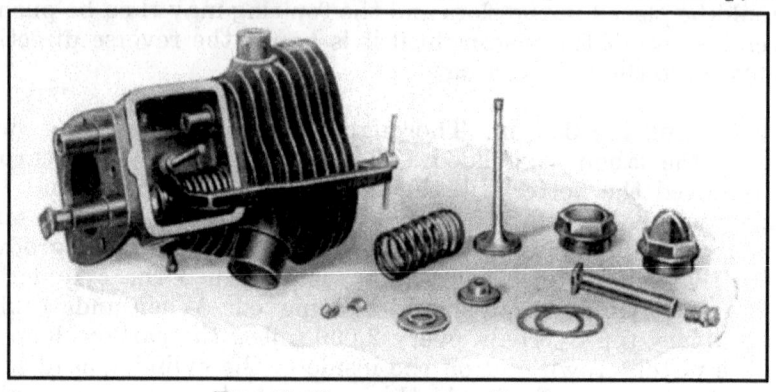

Fig. 43. Removing the Valves
(Model LB)

ended tool round their circumferences. Only a tool of the right size should be used, or the shape of the grooves may be spoiled.

Removing Valves (S.V. Models). Place the cylinder on its side—valve spring chamber upwards—on a bench, and remove the valves, using the valve extractor, which may be obtained from any of the Ariel agents. The forked end is placed under the valve collar and the point of the screw in the small centre hole in the valve head. Screw up, compressing the spring, and then remove the split cones. Unscrew the extractor and remove the valve, leaving the spring and collar in position resting on the tappet head. Both valves are dealt with in this manner. Fig. 43 shows the S.V. engine dismantled.

O.H.V. Models. The valves are held by the taper cotters and collars as in the side-valve model. The springs are easily removed by means of the special tool.

This tool is used as follows: Drop the square-shaped part through two of the head bolt holes and slip the wire through the small holes in the ends of the tool so that it cannot be withdrawn.

MAINTENANCE AND OVERHAULING

Place a small block of wood inside the head so that the valves rest on this, and then hold the head down firmly on the bench. With the two studs, which are inside the body of the tool, resting on the top spring collar, depress the handle, so compressing the spring, and withdraw the taper cotters. Note that the handle of the tool folds up if used the wrong way round. Having removed one valve (two on four-valve models), place the tool in the other two head bolt holes and remove the remaining valve(s) in a similar manner. Fig. 44 shows the valve remover in position.

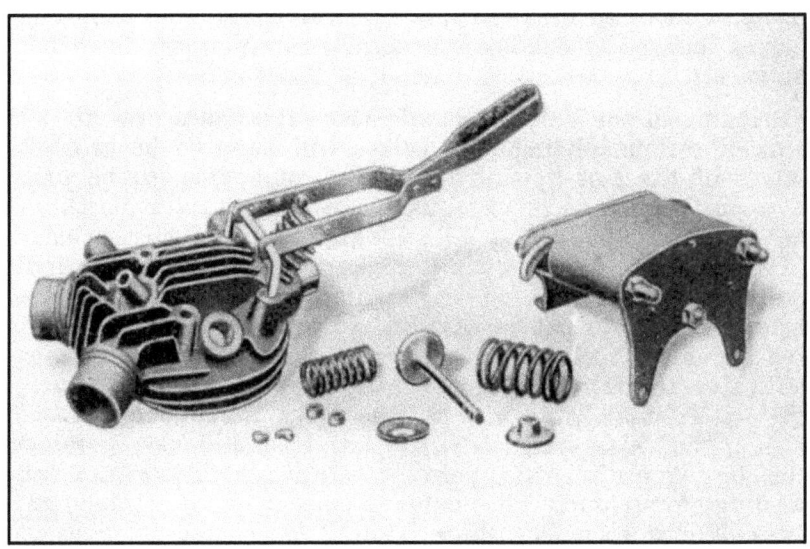

FIG. 44. REMOVING THE VALVES
(O.H.V. Lightweight Models)

O.H.C. Model. Take off the rocker-box cover and rotate the camshaft until all four valves belonging to the two front cylinders are on their seats. Remove the distributor cover back-plate, held by four screws; examination of the end face of the rocker-box behind the back-plate will show two holes in line with the two rocker spindles. Obtain a ¼-in. diameter bolt screwed 26 thds.-per-inch; insert this into the left-hand and screw it up into the end of the front rocker-spindle. Pulling this bolt outwards will pull the rocker-spindle out of the case and free the rockers, distance shims, and spring washers, etc. Carefully collect these as the spindle is pulled out and lay out each item on the bench in the same order. These parts are all interchangeable, but it is always better practice to replace a part in the same position, and if the items are, therefore, arranged on the bench in the sequence in which they come out, they can be put back into exactly the same order. The rear rocker, spindle is dealt with in exactly the same manner.

To remove the valves, get a small block of wood, small enough to fit inside the combustion chamber. Lay this block on the bench and place the head over it so that the top end of the block fits into one of the combustion chambers and bears up against two valve heads. Downward pressure on the top spring collar S (Fig. 38) will compress the valve spring, when the two split cones, or cotters, can be taken out. This releases the top collar and spring, which can be lifted off. The valve will then drop out as soon as the wood block is removed. Be careful not to interchange the valves.

Grinding-in the Valves. Should the valve faces or seats show signs of serious pitting, the valves will have to be ground-in. Valves of the side-by-side type have, of course, to be *pressed down* on their seatings when using a screwdriver, while those of the overhead type have to be *pulled up* against their seatings.

Only grind-in valves when necessary, using *fine* valve-grinding compound mixed with oil or paraffin; only a small quantity is necessary, and do not revolve the valves round and round, but give a quarter turn backwards and forwards, frequently raising the valve from its seat and dropping it down in a different positon. A small hand vice will be found a convenient tool for holding the valve stem on O.H.V. engines, and very great care must be taken after this operation to remove all traces of valve-grinding compound. The valve stems may be cleaned with *very fine* or worn emery cloth. Do not use coarse grinding compound for grinding valves in. A little fine paste smeared very lightly over the valve face is far better. Care should be taken to avoid burring the valve stems, otherwise unnecessary wear will take place in the valve guides. The same remarks apply to the head itself. This should be polished with very fine or used emery cloth after the deposit has been removed.

Do not grind valves unnecessarily, but see that all pit marks are removed from the valve face. Finish off with a fine powder. Wash cylinder, valve caps, and valve and springs, etc., in clean paraffin, taking great care to remove all traces of emery or grinding powder. Dry with a clean, smooth cloth. All is now ready for reassembling.

Reassembling (S.V. Engines). Before replacing see that all parts are perfectly clean, with no trace of emery powder from valve grinding and with no particles of carbon or dirt adhering to any of the internal parts.

When reassembling a side-valve engine, which is almost exactly

MAINTENANCE AND OVERHAULING 73

the dismantling process reversed, push gudgeon pin into the piston until it comes flush with inside of boss of piston; slip piston over connecting rod, then push gudgeon pin gently in. Refit the spring circlips. The piston rings should be spaced so that the gap of top ring faces front and gap of bottom ring faces rear. Smear piston thoroughly with oil and see that there is plenty behind the rings. Wipe top of the piston clean. The cylinder should be smeared with oil and then refitted to crankcase. If paper washer is torn, fit a new one. It should be smeared with seccotine or gold size.

If any difficulty is experienced in getting piston rings to enter cylinder, obtain assistance to hold the cylinder while the rings and piston are eased in. Before lowering the cylinder on certain models arrange the tappet "feet" fore and aft, and drop the cylinder into position. If the tappet "feet" are not arranged like this, they will not go into position on the cams. Screw down cylinder nuts, giving each a half-turn alternatively and diagonally. Fit the detachable head (all models except LB), taking care not to omit the copper-asbestos washer, and to re-tighten the cylinder fixing nuts evenly, finger tight first, and then with a spanner. Screw in sparking plug, refit exhaust lifter cable and the exhaust system. Attach valve cover, carburettor, and high-tension wire to plug. The work is now complete. Start engine and run gently until warm. Then check tappet clearances and cylinder and head holding-down nuts and bolts for tightness.

Reassembling (LF, MF, and MH). Make sure that the joint faces of the head and barrel are clean, smooth, and have no carbon particles or old jointing compound on them, or a tight joint will not be obtained (no jointing washer is used). See that the valves are closed. Smear the joint face on the barrel with a little of one of the special jointing compounds (goldsize may be used), place the head in position, and screw down the two offside head bolts finger tight. Replace the rocker-box, seeing that the ball ends on the rocker-arms are in the cups at the top ends of the push-rods, and that the enclosing tubes are located in the holes on the top of the return spring chamber. Insert the two set bolts securing the offside rocker-plate and then the two nearside head bolts. See that the four head-retaining bolts are turned down finger tight until the head of each bolt is down on to the cylinder head. Now take a spanner and give one bolt a one-sixth turn, repeat this on the bolt diagonally opposite, and then on the two remaining ones; keep going round in the same order, giving each bolt a one-sixth turn at a time until all are tight. This method ensures that the cylinder head is pulled down evenly so that a good joint is made. Remove the two link plates.

The following applies to all O.H.V. models: *it is important to remember to replace the hardened steel cap ends on the valve stems or considerable damage may be done.*

Models VG, VH, and SG. Rotate the engine until neither cam lever is on the lift, i.e. valves closed. See that all parts are clean and free from grinding paste, make sure that the joint faces of the head and barrel are clean, smooth, and have no carbon particles or old jointing compound on them, or a tight joint will not be obtained (no jointing washer is used). Smear the joint face on the barrel with a little of one of the special jointing compounds (goldsize may be used), place the head in position and screw down the head bolts finger tight, and then give one bolt a one-sixth turn. Going round clockwise, repeat this on the *next but one* bolt, and so on round the head, missing one bolt each time and tightening the bolt *next but one* to the one just tightened.

Insert the two push-rods into their enclosing tubes, seeing that the oil baffle assembly is in position at the top end of each rod. Put the rods and covers into position with the ball ends of the locating rods with the cups in the cam levers. If the rubber jointing washers are damaged or perished, fit new ones, or an oil leak will occur. Place the hardened steel caps on the valve stems. Take the rocker-box, replace the exhaust lifter wire if this has been removed, and put the box into position, seeing that the ball ends on the rocker-arms are in the cups at the top of the push-rods, and that the enclosing tubes are located in the recessed portion at the base of the rocker-box. Keep the rocker-box pressed down so as to overcome the resistance due to the compression of the rubber washers at the bottom of the push-rod tubes, and insert the two set bolts which secure the rocker-box to the pillars on the timing side. Make sure that these set bolts are screwed in straight or the thread will be damaged: due to the upward thrust on the rocker-box, it is easy to get the threads crossed if a little care is not exercised. Tighten up these set bolts and secure the other side of the box with the two nuts which screw on the tops of the head bolts. Replace the carburettor, sparking plug, silencing system, etc.

O.H.C. Models. The reassembly of the head, etc., of the Square Four is perfectly straightforward. Assuming that the valves have been replaced and the rocker gear assembled, the head and rocker box is now complete and ready for replacing on the cylinder block. See that all trace of jointing compound has been scraped away from the joint face on the head, and that the gaskets are in sound condition.

On 1932 models, four gaskets are used instead of the one big one on earlier types. These gaskets are copper faced on each

MAINTENANCE AND OVERHAULING

side and can therefore be used either way up (on earlier types the steel face should be placed next to the head, with the brass face next to the block). Be particularly careful, however, to see that each gasket is replaced with its greatest diameter truly across the cylinder bore, so that it matches up with the oval shape of the combustion chamber.

Should a gasket require renewing at any time, a complete set of four pieces *must* be used. The gaskets are graded and arranged in sets, which must not be split.

Smear the exposed faces of the gaskets with jointing compound and drop the head down on to the cylinder block, screwing the four nuts on to the head-retaining studs and inserting the four head bolts. To do this, first see that the four head bolt and stud nuts are screwed up so that they are resting on the faces of the bosses.

Screw the head bolts down finger tight, taking care to do the outer bolts first. The

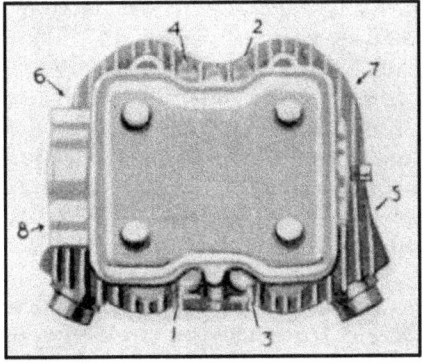

FIG. 45. ORDER OF TIGHTENING HEAD BOLTS AND NUTS

correct order of tightening up the bolts on 1932 machines is as follows: 5, 6, 7, 8, 1, 2, 3, 4. (See Fig. 45.) This tends to bring the greatest pressure on the outer edges of the gaskets, a result which materially assists in getting a good gastight joint.

If the fibre washers which make the joint between the rocker box and the chain case are damaged, they must be replaced before the head is fitted. To re-fit the camshaft sprocket on the camshaft it is necessary, on the 1932 models, to take off the outer camshaft chain case cover. First, unscrew the sprocket extractor bolt and withdraw the bolt and collar; the sprocket will drop down on to the edge of the camshaft bearing housing and will remain there, keeping the chain properly in mesh with the sprockets whilst the chain cover is taken off.

Now press the tension spring up against the side of the chain case, placing the bolt *M* (Fig. 40) through the sprocket and lightly screw it up into the crank shaft. Rotate the engine slowly, pressing the sprocket inwards against the camshaft until the sprocket key engages with the camshaft key-way. Now tighten up the bolt *M*, and replace the chain cover.

The valve timing cannot possibly be assembled incorrectly if these instructions are carried out, as there is only one key in the sprocket and one key-way in the camshaft. Replace the sprocket inspection nut, the rocker box oil pipe, the rocker box cover and joint washer, and do up the oil gauge pipe connection. Be careful with the cover joint washer, seeing that this is properly in position before doing up the securing nuts tightly, so that a good oil retaining joint may be made. Now fit the exhaust pipes, carburettor, sparking plugs, and distributor cover, and connect the leads to the appropriate plugs. The engine should then be ready for starting.

When a gasket is first fitted, it will " give," or compress freely as the engine warms up. Therefore, when the engine has been run from 10 to 15 minutes, tighten the head bolts again. Repeat this in about 50 miles and again after a similar distance. This should pull the gasket down to its compression limit. A periodical testing of the holding down bolts will prevent any possibility of a blown gasket. Before pulling down the head, the camshaft case screws Q (Fig. 40) should be slackened off and, of course, subsequently re-tightened.

Dismantling the Timing Gear (Models LB, LF, MB, MF, and MH). Undo the ten cheese-headed screws securing the chain cover and remove this. Undo the nuts holding the magneto driving sprockets and withdraw the sprockets with the extractor provided. It is unnecessary to remove the oil pump, and this is best left in position. Now undo the single cheese-head screw by the magneto driving sprocket, and withdraw the gear cover, pressing on the ends of the camshaft spindles to prevent these being pulled out and the timing upset. Note that the cover is located on the crank case face by means of two hollow pegs.

If the cams are removed, it is perfectly easy to reset the timing. Rotate the engine until the piston is towards the top of the cylinder. The timing pinion will be seen to be centre-punched in two places: one dot towards the top left and two dots towards the top right; take the inlet cam, lift the tappet, and insert the cam wheel so that the centre dot marked on this coincides with the single dot on the pinion. Similarly, insert the exhaust cam, which has two dots on the timing pinion.

Note that the dots on the timing pinion are sometimes covered up by the securing nut; this nut has a left-hand thread. It is impossible to get the timing wrong if these instructions are carried out carefully. The timing pinion has one keyway and the mainshaft is keyed to the fly-wheel.

Be careful to replace all joint washers, renewing these if damaged, and securely screw up all nuts, etc., or an oil leak may occur. It is most important to note that, when securing the timing cover, the paper washer must be replaced in position, and

MAINTENANCE AND OVERHAULING

that there is an *additional paper washer* ·005 in. thick at the joint connection to the sump.

Models VB, VG, and VH. Undo the seven set-screws securing the chain cover and remove this. Remove the oil pump by taking out the two cheese-headed screws. Next undo the nuts holding

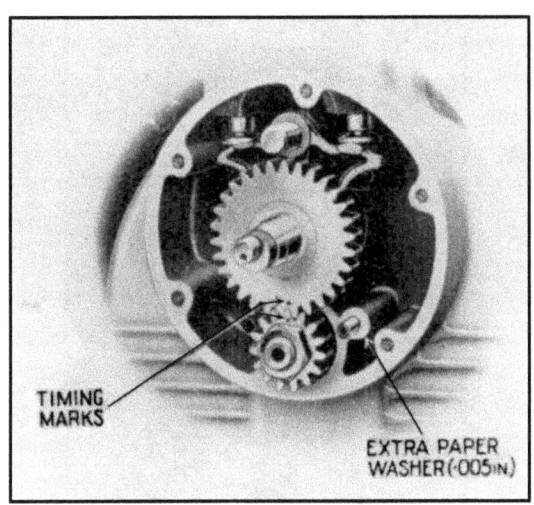

Fig. 46. The Timing Gear
(Models VB, VG, and VH)

the magneto driving sprockets and withdraw the sprockets with the extractor provided. Before removing the sprocket behind the oil pump, slip the small adaptor on to the eccentric on the end of the spindle. This prevents damage to this part. Undo the two oil pipes to the oil tank, that to the chain, and the small one to the oil gauge. This latter is at the front of the case. Now slack off the set-bolt holding the magneto platform and remove the five set-screws securing the timing cover. Withdraw the gear cover, pressing on the end of the camshaft spindle to prevent this being pulled out and the timing upset.

If the cams are removed, the timing is perfectly easily reset. Rotate the engine until the piston is at top dead centre. The timing pinion and cam wheel will be seen to be centre-punched. Take the cam wheel, lift the cam levers, and insert the cam wheel so that the centre dot marked on this coincides with the centre dot on the pinion (see Fig. 46). Sometimes the dot on the timing pinion is covered up by the nut (left-hand thread).

When fitting the cam levers, insert that for the inlet valve first, and then that for the exhaust valve. The small hole in the lever for lubricating the cam lever pin bearing comes on top.

It is impossible to get the timing wrong if these instructions are carried out carefully. The timing pinion has one keyway and the mainshaft is keyed to the fly-wheel.

Be careful to replace all joint washers, renewing these if

Fig. 47. Timing Gear, Showing Decompressor, as Fitted on Models SB and SG

(The engine here depicted is the SG)

damaged, and securely do up all nuts, screws, etc., or an oil leak may occur. Here again it is most important to note that when replacing the timing cover, the paper washer must be in position and that there is an *additional paper washer* ·005 in. thick at the joint connection to the sump. Do not forget the set bolt supporting the magneto platform.

Models SB, SG. Disconnect the oil gauge pipe and then take off the timing cover after undoing the ten set-screws holding the cover to the case. Undo the nut which secures the magneto sprocket to the armature shaft and draw the pinion off the paper

MAINTENANCE AND OVERHAULING 79

on the shaft by means of the extractor provided in the tool kit. The idler wheel simply slides off the spindle. If the engine is rotated so that both the valves are closed, the cam wheel can also be pulled out.

The timing pinion is a light driving fit on the mainshaft and is tightened up by means of the locking nut—left-hand thread—against a shoulder. The pinion is keyed so that it can only be fitted in one position. The radiused end of the hole through the pinion goes up against the shoulder on the shaft. A centre-punch mark will be noted by one of the teeth on the timing pinion, and there is a corresponding mark on the cam wheel. When the teeth are meshed so that these two dots come opposite one another, the valve timing is correct (see Fig. 47). When fitting the cam levers, insert that for the inlet valve first, and then for the exhaust valve. The small hole in the lever for lubricating the cam lever pin bearing comes on top.

When replacing the cover, see that the joint washer is not damaged or broken, and securely do up the retaining screws or an oil leak will occur.

The Decompressor. The latest SB and SG Ariel machines have decompressors fitted to the timing case to facilitate starting. The decompressor cam, which lifts the exhaust valve during a part of the compression stroke, is mounted on the engine mainshaft at the back of the timing pinion. The decompressor lever is mounted on an eccentric and can be brought into action by the partial rotation of the eccentric spindle.

The spindle is actuated through the medium of the outer lever and is held in position by friction. This friction is obtained by the compression of a coil spring mounted on the spindle and compressed between the end of the eccentric and the inner end of the timing cover bearing.

It will probably be found that when the machine has been on the road some little time, parts will bed down, so reducing the friction, with the result that the outer lever will drop instead of remaining in the " up " position, when the engine is kicked over with the decompressor in action. This is easily rectified by fitting a packing washer on the eccentric spindle between the spring and the bearing. To fit this washer, undo the nut holding the outer lever and take this off. Do not disturb the flange bearing plate. Now take off the timing cover, pressing on the end of the eccentric spindle, in order not to upset the lifter parts, etc. Fit the washer and replace the cover.

O.H.C. Model. The timing gear for this model is perfectly simple, and absolutely straightforward in replacement if a few simple instructions are carried out. The actual 2 to 1 reduction between the engine crankshaft and the camshaft is brought about by the small gear on the front crankshaft meshing with the larger gear on the half-time shaft. The large gear engages with the boss up against the shoulder on the half-time shaft. These two gears are inside the centre gearcase. The half-time shaft has one plain bearing in the wall at this centre gearcase, and the other bearing (a ball) in the wall of the outer gearcase. Keyed on to the outer end of the half-time shaft is the magneto driving sprocket and then the camshaft driving sprocket. The large sprocket, i.e. the magneto driving sprocket, fits with the small boss inside, while the camshaft driving sprocket should also be put on with the boss inwards.

The camshaft sprocket is keyed and bolted to the end of the camshaft and has the same number of teeth as the driving sprocket, the reduction having already been brought about by the half-time gears. These two timing pinions inside the main gearcase are keyed to their respective shafts, whilst the two sprockets already mentioned are also keyed to their shafts. The valve timing is therefore fixed, except for the variation brought about by altering the mesh of the interior timing gears, or by altering the mesh of the two chain sprockets with the camshaft chain. To get accurate adjustment of the valve timing when first assembling the engine, a vernier arrangement is incorporated in the camshaft sprocket. During the ordinary course of reassembly, that is to say, so long as the reduction gears inside the centre gearcase are not disturbed, it is quite unnecessary to disturb the vernier setting. Assemble the half-time shaft sprocket, rotate the engine until No. 1 piston is at top dead centre, and then turn the camshaft clockwise, when looked at from the driving end, until the inlet valve of No. 1 cylinder has just commenced to open (this valve commences to open with the crank 10° before top dead centre). Slip the camshaft sprocket into position on the end of the camshaft so that the key is engaging with the keyway, slip the chain on to the lower sprocket, taking care not to rotate the engine, and pull the chain up into position. It will then be found that the teeth on the camshaft sprocket are in line with the side-plates on the chain; that is, the chain and the sprocket are ready to mesh. Mark one of the teeth of the camshaft sprocket and the corresponding side-plate of the chain, slip the sprocket off the camshaft, insert it into the chain, so that the marked tooth is in mesh with the marked link, and then slip the sprocket back on to the camshaft and tighten up with the centre bolt. If the instructions have been followed out correctly, the timing will be right.

Reassembling in this manner, without touching the vernier

MAINTENANCE AND OVERHAULING

adjustment means that the timing will either be correct, or one or more complete teeth out. Following the instructions as given brings the timing right.

VALVE TIMING

Model	Inlet Opens	Inlet Closes	Exhaust Opens	Exhaust Closes
LB, LF	$\frac{1}{64}$ in. or 5° before T.D.C.	$\frac{7}{16}$ in. or 50° after B.D.C.	$\frac{33}{64}$ in. or 55° before B.D.C.	$\frac{7}{64}$ in. or 20° after T.D.C.
MB, MF, MH	5° before T.D.C.	$\frac{15}{32}$ in. or 50° after B.D.C.	$\frac{37}{64}$ in. or 55° before B.D.C.	$\frac{1}{8}$ in. or 20° after T.D.C.
VG, VH, SG	$\frac{9}{64}$ in. or 22° before T.D.C.	$\frac{15}{16}$ in. or 70° after B.D.C.	$\frac{15}{16}$ in. or 70° before B.D.C.	$\frac{3}{16}$ in. or 25° after T.D.C.
VB, SB	$\frac{1}{64}$ in. or 5° before T.D.C.	$\frac{17}{32}$ in. or 50° after B.D.C.	$\frac{5}{8}$ in. or 55° before B.D.C.	$\frac{5}{32}$ in. or 20° after T.D C
4F	$\frac{1}{32}$ in. or 10° before T.D.C.	$\frac{11}{32}$ in. or 50° after B.D.C.	$\frac{13}{32}$ in. or 55° before B.D.C.	$\frac{3}{64}$ in. or 15° after T.D.C.

Retiming the Magneto (Models LB, LF, MB, MF, MH, VB, VG, VH). Remove the sparking plug and release the magneto sprocket from the taper on the armature shaft. Rotate the engine until the piston is at top dead centre and both valves are closed. Set the ignition control " full retard." Move the contact-breaker in the direction of rotation until the points are just separating, and tighten up the chain sprocket, taking care that this operation does not alter the setting. It is advisable to check the setting because of its importance. This setting gives approximately $\frac{7}{16}$ in. advance before top dead centre.

With the models MH, VG, and VH give slightly more advance. Set the contact-breaker points just separating with the cam ring at full advance, and the piston approximately $\frac{1}{2}$ in. or $\frac{9}{16}$ in. before top dead centre.

If a Maglita, running at engine speed, is fitted, time as follows: Set the piston $\frac{7}{16}$ in. *before* top dead centre with the piston coming up the compression stroke; this brings both valves closed. Set the contact-breaker cam ring at *full advance* and the points just breaking.

Models SB, SG. Remove the sparking plug and take off the timing cover (do not forget to disconnect the oil gauge pipe at the top of the cover). Release the magneto pinion from the taper on the armature shaft. Rotate the engine until the piston is at top dead centre and *both valves are closed*. Set the ignition control to "full retard." Move the contact-breaker in the direction of rotation until the points are just separating, and tighten up the pinion, taking care that this operation does not alter the setting. This should be checked. The setting gives approximately $\frac{7}{16}$ in. advance before top dead centre.

Model 4F. To retime the magneto on this model, take out the sparking plug from No. 1 cylinder and remove the plug V (Fig. 31). Undo the nut holding the magneto sprocket to the armature. Screw the extractor into the thread cut in the sprocket box and then screw the set pin through the centre of the extractor. As soon as this pin comes up against the end of the armature shaft it will free the sprocket from the taper. The extractor can be withdrawn and the sprocket will remain in position on the armature. Now, rotating the engine in its normal direction, bring the piston of No. 1 cylinder up to within $\frac{5}{16}$ in. of top dead centre with both valves closed. The distributor centre piece on the end of the camshaft should be pointing to approximately 7 hr. 30 min. Remove the magneto contact-breaker cover, see that the ignition control is in the fully advanced position, and rotate the magneto contact-breaker anti-clockwise (looked at from the contact-breaker end) until the points just begin to separate. Take a box spanner, place it up against the face of the magneto sprocket and give the outer end of the spanner a sharp tap. This will drive the sprocket up on to the armature taper and will hold the sprocket in position whilst the retaining nut is being done up tightly. Replace the sparking plug, and the plug V in the chain cover. It is always a sound plan to check the timing after tightening the sprocket securing nut, just to make quite certain that the sprocket has not slipped during the tightening up operation.

CARBURETTOR MAINTENANCE

Tuning the Amal Carburettor. Should the setting of this instrument not give entire satisfaction for particular requirements, there are four separate ways of rectifying matters as given herewith, and the adjustment should be made in this order: (*a*) Main jet (three-quarters to full throttle); (*b*) Pilot air adjustment (closed to one-eighth throttle); (*c*) Throttle valve cut-away on the air-intake side (one-eighth to one-quarter throttle); (*d*) Needle position (one-quarter to three-quarters throttle). The diagram (Fig. 48) clearly indicates the part of the throttle range over which each adjustment is offective.

(*a*) To obtain the correct main jet size, several jets should be experimented with, and that selected should be the *smallest which gives maximum power and speed on full throttle.*

(*b*) To weaken slow-running mixture, screw pilot air adjuster outwards, and to enrich screw pilot air adjuster inwards.

Screw pilot air adjuster home in a clockwise direction. Place gear lever in "neutral." Slightly flood the float chamber by gently depressing the tickler until fuel begins to escape from the mixing chamber. Set magneto at half advance, throttle approximately one-eighth open, close the air lever, start the engine, and warm up. After warming up, reduce the engine revolutions by gently throttling down. The slow-running mixture will prove over-rich unless air leaks exist. Very gradually unscrew the pilot jet adjuster. The engine speed will increase, and must again be reduced by gently closing the throttle until, by a combination of throttle position and air adjustment, the desired "idling" is obtained. It is occasionally necessary to retard completely the magneto before getting a satisfactory tick-over, especially when early ignition timing is used. If it is desired to make the engine idle with the throttle quite closed, the position of the throttle valve must be set by means of the throttle stop-screw, the throttle

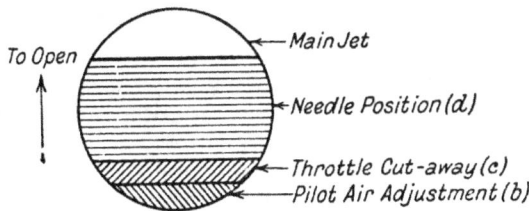

FIG. 48. RANGE AND SEQUENCE OF ADJUSTMENTS — AMAL CARBURETTOR

lever during this adjustment being pushed right home. Alternatively, if the screw is adjusted clear of the throttle valve, the engine will be shut off in the normal way by the control lever.

(c) Given satisfactory "tick-over," set the magneto control at half-advance with the air lever fully open. Very slowly open the throttle valve when, if the engine responds regularly up to one-quarter throttle, the valve cut-away is correct.

A weak mixture is indicated by spitting back through the air-intake with blue flames and hesitation in picking up, which disappears when the air lever is closed down. This can be remedied by fitting a throttle valve with less cut-away. A rich mixture is shown by a black, sooty exhaust, and the engine falters when the air valve is closed. The remedy for this is a throttle valve with greater cut-away. Each Amal valve is stamped with two numbers, the first indicating the type number of the carburettor, and the second figure the amount of cut-away on the intake side of the valve in sixteenths of an inch, e.g. 6/4 is a type 6 valve with four-sixteenths in a $\frac{1}{4}$ in. cut-away.

(d) Open air lever fully and the throttle half-way. Note if the exhaust is crisp and the engine flexible. Close the air valve slightly below the throttle, when the exhaust note and engine revolutions should remain constant. Should popping back and spitting occur with blue flames from the intake, the mixture is weak, and the needle should be slightly raised. Test by lowering the air valve gently. The engine revolutions will rise when the air valve is lowered slightly below the throttle valve.

If the engine speed does not increase progressively with raising of the throttle, and a smoky exhaust is apparent with heavy laboured running, and tendency to eight-stroke, the mixture is too rich and the needle should be lowered in the throttle valve. Having found the correct needle position, the carburettor setting is now complete, and it will be found that the driving is practically automatic once the engine is warmed up. For speed work the main jet may be increased by 10 per cent, when the air lever should be fully open on full throttle.

Cleaning the Amal Carburettor. Periodical cleaning is necessary to maintain efficient functioning of the carburettor, and should be carried out in the following sequence—

Disconnect petrol pipe. Unscrew holding bolt Q (Fig. 26) and remove float chamber complete. With box or set spanner, slacken the mixing chamber union nut E. Mixing chamber complete may now be removed from engine, either by unscrewing the clip pin (if outlet) or the bolts (if flange fitting). Unscrew mixing chamber lock ring, and pull out throttle valve needle and air valve. Remove main jet P and needle jet O. Mixing chamber union nut E may then be removed and jet block complete pushed out. If this is obstinate, tap gently, using a wooden stump inside the mixing chamber. Unscrew float chamber cover W and slacken lock screw X. Withdraw the float by pinching the clip V inwards, and at the same time pull gently upwards.

Generally it is sufficient to wash all the parts in clean petrol, but if the carburettor has had extended service, check the following—

(*a*) FLOAT CHAMBER NEEDLE U. If a distinct shoulder is visible on the point of seating, renew this as soon as convenient.

(*b*) THROTTLE VALVE. Test in mixing chamber, and if excessive play is present it is advisable to renew this without delay.

(*c*) THROTTLE NEEDLE CLIP. This part must securely grip needle. *Free rotation must not take place*, otherwise the needle groove will become worn and necessitate a new part being fitted. *Be sure to refit the clip in the same groove.*

(*d*) JET BLOCK. If trouble has been experienced with erratic "idling," ascertain by means of a fine bristle that the pilot jet J is clear, and that the pilot outlet M in the mixing chamber is unobstructed.

To Reassemble. Refit jet block F with washer on underside, and screw on lightly mixing chamber union nut E. Screw in needle jet O and main jet P. Open air lever $\frac{7}{8}$ in., throttle lever half-way; grasp the air slide between the thumb and the finger; *make sure that the needle enters the central hole in the adaptor top.* Slightly twist the throttle valve until it enters the adaptor guide, when on pushing down the valves the air valve should enter its guide. If not, slightly move the mixing chamber top, when the air valve will slide into place. Screw on mixing chamber lock-nut. *No brute force is necessary.*

Attach carburettor to the cylinder, pushing right home, and examine washer if flange fitting. Insert holding bolt Q, and thoroughly tighten union nut E by means of a fixed spanner. Refit float and needle, holding the needle head against its seating by means of a pencil until the float and the clip V are slipped into position. Make sure that the clip enters the groove provided. Screw on the cover tightly and lock in position by means of the lock screw X. Fit holding bolt in float chamber with one washer above and one below the lug. Screw holding bolt into mixing chamber and lock securely. Clean petrol pipe and filter if fitted, and replace. It will be necessary to re-check the pilot setting if this has been disturbed.

DYNAMO MAINTENANCE

Before removing the cover for any reason, it is advisable to disconnect the positive lead of the battery to avoid the danger of reversing the polarity of the dynamo or short-circuiting the battery, either of which might cause serious damage.

If at any time a " Magdyno " equipped motor-cycle must be ridden with the batteries disconnected, or in any way out of service, it is essential to run with the switch in the " OFF " position.

With the "Maglita" the lamps, in case of emergency, can be run direct off the generator, by disconnecting the battery and turning the control switch to the full "on" position. Under these circumstances the engine speed should be kept down below about 2,500 r.p.m., as otherwise the lamps may burn out. Never run the generator direct with the switch in the "dim" position, as this is likely to burn out both the pilot and tail bulbs. If direct running is necessary, put the control switch to full "on" either before starting up or while the engine is turning over very slowly. Always turn the control switch to the "off" position after stopping the engine, as this prevents the possible discharging of the battery in the event of the cut-out sticking.

Brushes. It is very important to make sure that the brushes work freely in their holders. This can be easily ascertained by holding back the spring lever and gently pulling each flexible lead, when the brush should move without the slightest suggestion of sluggishness. It should also return to its original position directly the lead is let go. When testing the brush in this way, release it gently, otherwise it may get chipped. The brushes should be clean and "bed" over the whole surface; that is, the face in contact with the commutator segments should appear

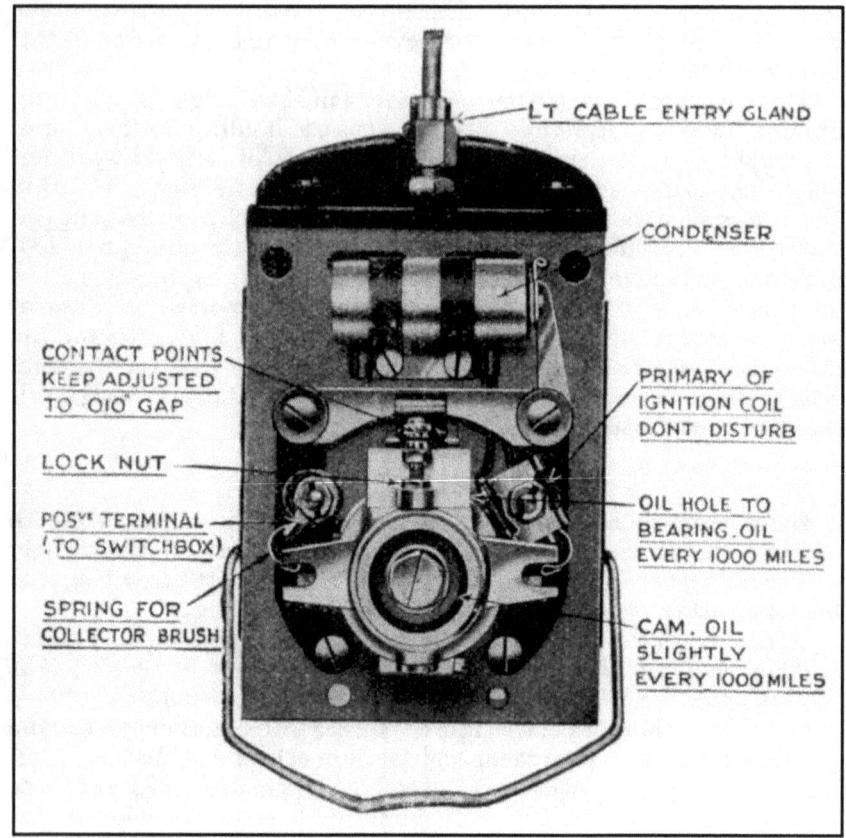

Fig. 49. Contact-breaker Side of F.D. "Maglita," Showing Some Points Requiring Attention

uniformly polished. Dirty brushes may be cleaned with a cloth moistened with petrol.

The brush springs should be inspected occasionally to see that they have sufficient tension to keep the brushes firmly pressed against the commutator when the machine is running. It is particularly necessary to keep this in mind when the brushes have been in use a long time and are very much worn down. Do not insert brushes of a grade other than that supplied with the machine, and do not change the tension springs. It is advisable to inspect the brushes about every 3,000 miles.

MAINTENANCE AND OVERHAULING

Commutator. The surface of the commutator should be kept clean and free from oil or brush dust, etc. Should any grease or oil work its way on to the commutator through over-lubrication, it will not only cause sparking, but, in addition, carbon and copper dust will be collected in the grooves between the commutator segments. The best way to clean the commutator is, without disconnecting any leads, to remove from its box one of the main brushes and, inserting a fine duster in the box, hold it, by means of a suitably-shaped piece of wood, against the commutator surface, causing the armature to be rotated at the same time.

Electromagnetic Cut-out. The cut-out automatically closes, by means of solenoids, the charging circuit as soon as the dynamo voltage rises above that of the battery. When the dynamo voltage falls below that of the battery the reverse action takes place; that is, the cut-out opens and thereby prevents the battery from discharging itself through the dynamo.

The cut-out is accurately set before leaving the works, and should not be tampered with or adjusted. Should the cut-out fail to close the circuit on accelerating the engine, the cause of the damage is likely to be found elsewhere. There is no such relation between the operation of the cut-out and the state of charge of the battery.

Absence of Fuses. In order to simplify the system as far as possible, no fuse is provided. If all the connections are kept clean and tight, there is no possibility of any excess current causing damage to the apparatus.

Lubrication. The armature bearings are packed with grease by the manufacturers and require no attention until a big mileage has been covered, when it is desirable to return a "Magdyno" or "Maglita" to a Lucas Service Department for cleaning and re-lubricating.

A Warning. On no account attempt to remove the dynamo armature unless this is done by a person having sound electrical knowledge, as de-magnetization of the magnets will probably be caused.

CARE OF LAMPS

Cleaning Reflectors. The reflectors are protected by a transparent and colourless covering, which enables any accidental finger marks to be removed with a soft cloth or chamois leather without affecting the surface of the reflectors. On no account should a metal polish be used on Lucas reflectors, as this is liable to ruin the surfaces. If the ebony black of the outer body becomes dull in service, the original lustre can be restored by the application of a little good furniture or car polish.

Focusing Headlamp. The best method of focusing is to take the motor-cycle to a straight, level road, find the correct bulb adjustment, and then move the lamp in its adjustable mounting until the best road position is obtained. The driving light should be switched on when focusing is carried out. Special care should be taken to see that the filament is in its correct position relative to the reflector.

Replacement of Bulbs. Always use Lucas bulbs with Lucas reflectors. When it is found necessary to replace the main headlamp bulb, screw it out two or three turns in an anti-clockwise direction. This will release the pressure on the bulb contacts and enable the bulb to be withdrawn easily. Care should be taken that the bulb is fitted the correct way round, i.e. with the dipped beam filament above the centre filament. Spare bulbs are best carried in a Lucas bulb case.

CARE OF THE BATTERY

It is of the utmost importance that the battery should receive regular attention to keep it in good condition.

The following are the most important maintenance hints—
1. Keep the acid level $\frac{1}{4}$ in. above the top of the plates.
2. Add only distilled water, never tap water.
3. Test the condition of the battery by taking readings of the specific gravity of the acid with a hydrometer.
4. The battery must never be left in a discharged condition.

Topping-up. At least once a month the vent plugs in the top of the battery should be removed and the level of the acid solution examined. If necessary, distilled water, which can be obtained at all chemists and most garages, should be added to bring the level above the tops of the plates, but well short of the bottom of the vent plugs. If, however, acid solution has been spilled, it should be replaced by a diluted sulphuric acid solution of specific gravity, 1·285. It is important when examining the cells that naked lights should not be held near the vents, on account of the possible danger of igniting the gas coming from the plates.

Storage. If the equipment is laid by for several months, the battery must be given a small charge from a separate source of electrical energy about once a fortnight, in order to obviate any permanent sulphation of the plates. In no circumstances must the electrolyte be removed from the battery and the plates allowed to dry, as certain chemical changes take place which result in permanent loss of capacity.

Testing the Condition of the Battery. It is advisable to complete the inspection by measuring the specific gravity of the acid, as this gives a very good indication of the state of charge of the battery.

An instrument known as a "hydrometer" is employed for this purpose. These can be bought at any Lucas Service Depot. Voltmeter readings of each cell do not provide a reliable indication of the condition of the battery, unless special precautions are taken.

Battery-charging Period. It is difficult to lay down rigid instructions on this subject, as the conditions under which motorcycles are used vary considerably; and, obviously, the amount of charging a battery will require is directly dependent on the

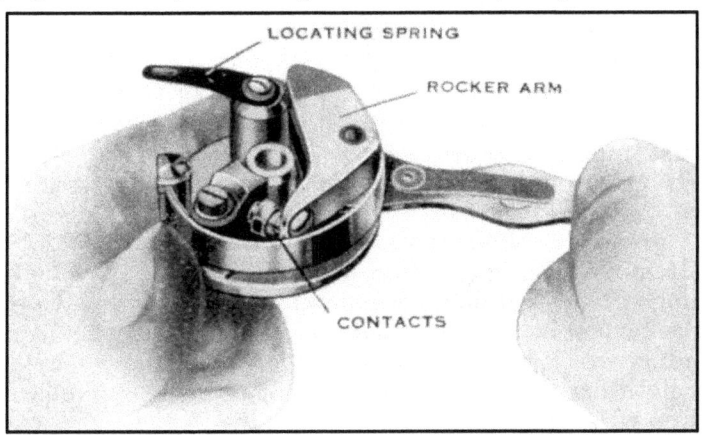

FIG. 50. REMOVAL OF LUCAS CONTACT-BREAKER ROCKER-ARM

extent to which the lamps are used. The following suggestions will serve as a rough guide—

The switch should be left in the C position for about 1 hour daily. This time should only be increased if the period of night running is considerable, or when the battery is found to be in a low state of charge (if the specific gravity of the acid solution is 1·210 or below). The chief ill-effect of overcharging is loss of acid by gassing.

The battery must never be left in a fully-discharged condition, and unless some long runs are to be taken, it is advisable to have the battery removed from the machine and charged up from an independent electrical supply.

Care of the Lucas Magneto (or Magneto Portion of "Magdyno"). When undertaking an annual overhaul, the following points should be attended to—

(*a*) Polish the contacts—if of tungsten, with fine emery cloth; if platinum, with a dead smooth file. To render the points accessible for cleaning, it is necessary to withdraw the contact-breaker from its housing by unscrewing the hexagon-headed retaining screw by means of the magneto spanner. The whole contact-breaker can then be pulled off the tapered shaft on which it fits. Now push aside the locating spring and prise the rocker-arm off its bearing, as shown in Fig. 50, when it will be possible to begin cleaning the points. Do not interfere with the spring-retaining screws. Before removing the rocker-arm, note whether the breaking of the contacts is at all sluggish by putting pressure on the fibre heel. If this is found to be the case, the bearing pin should be cleaned with very fine emery cloth and afterwards moistened with a little oil. When replacing the contact-breaker, care should be taken to ensure that the projecting key on the tapered portion of the contact-breaker base engages with the key-way cut in the armature spindle, or the whole timing of the magneto will be upset. The hexagon-headed screw should be tightened up with care; it must not be too slack (for it is part of the primary circuit), nor must undue force be used.

(b) If the machine has done a season's riding, remove the driving end bearing plate and resoak the felt washer in good quality grease or replace with a new one.

(c) Remove the high-tension pick-up by swinging aside the flat retaining spring, and polish the moulding with a clean cloth. See that the carbon brush is working freely in its holder and that it is not unduly worn. Clean the slip-ring track and flanges by holding a soft cloth damped with petrol by means of a piece of wood on the ring while the engine is being slowly and very carefully rotated. A magneto run with a carbon brush absent or sticking produces nitric acid internally (due to the sparking), which destroys all the lubricant, and attacks both the metal and insulation of which the armature is composed. If the brush is accidentally broken, care must be taken that no pieces are allowed to remain inside, or serious damage will result.

(d) Examine the high-tension cable, and replace if the rubber shows signs of disintegrating.

(e) See that the contacts "break" to the correct extent (·012 in.). It is seldom necessary, nor is it desirable, to dismantle the magneto. The armature of a magneto cannot be removed without loss of magnetism from the magnet and, unless facilities for remagnetizing are available, it is best not to dismantle. If you must dismantle, first remove the pick-up and the safety spark screw, or a broken slip-ring may result.

Care of the M-L Magneto. The handling of the M-L magneto is very similar to that of the Lucas just described; but, of course, the contact-breaker mechanism is of different design. Special care should be taken to see that the action of the vertical tappet is quite free.

MAINTENANCE AND OVERHAULING 91

Dismantling Lucas Spring Magneto Control. Should it become necessary at any time to dismantle the spring control and Bowden cable, proceed as follows: First remove the contact-breaker cover, held in position by a spring arm, and then withdraw the cam ring. Next, unscrew the fixing screw, which is sunk flush with the surface of the end plate. Finally pull the Bowden cable until it comes right out, together with the cable stop (which screws into the end plate), lock-nut, end plate, and plunger.

Removing Bowden Cable from M-L Magneto. To remove the cable from the instrument, do not attempt to remove the cam from its housing. It is only necessary to undo the hexagon nut which forms the abutment for the outer casing of the Bowden cable. If the cable and plunger to which it is attached are drawn upwards to their fullest extent, it will be found that the nipple into which the end of the cable is soldered comes above the top of the boss on the cam cage housing. The nipple may then be slipped sideways out of the hole in the plunger in which it fits, thus detaching the cable entirely.

CHAPTER VII

WHEELS AND TYRES

EVERY motor-cyclist naturally wants to get as many miles out of his tyres as is possible with safety. The tyres on an Ariel are of large section, and should therefore last for a very considerable time. It has been mentioned in Chapter II that the life of a rear and front tyre on a solo machine should be 6,000 and 10,000 miles

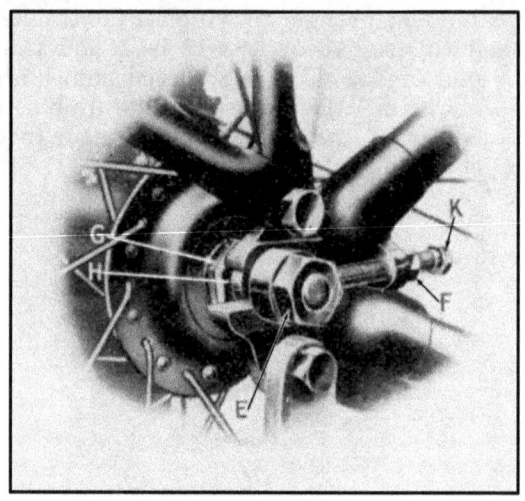

FIG. 51. PROVISION FOR REAR WHEEL AND
CHAIN ADJUSTMENT

K—Adjusting screw
F—Lock nut
G—Cone adjusting nut
H—Cone adjusting lock nut
E—Spindle nut

respectively, those of a sidecar machine being as follows: rear 5,000, front 8,000, sidecar indefinite, say, 20,000.

If the tyres and the machine itself receive proper attention the former should last these distances without difficulty, and in some cases very much greater mileages may be obtained. If the tyres, however, are misused or the machine is run with the wheels out of line, excessive wear will take place.

The greatest thief of tyre life is misalignment of wheels, and the rider would be well advised to check this alignment from time to time. This can easily be done on a solo machine with the aid of a straight piece of wood and on a sidecar machine with two similar pieces of wood.

It is, of course, absolutely essential that the edge of the board should be dead straight and square, and that it should be at least as long as the machine itself. Let us take the case of the solo motor-cycle first. Put the machine on the stand and place the straight edge of the board alongside the two wheels, as high up as possible. Then turn the front wheel until the board touches both sides of the front tyre and at least one side of the rear tyre. If

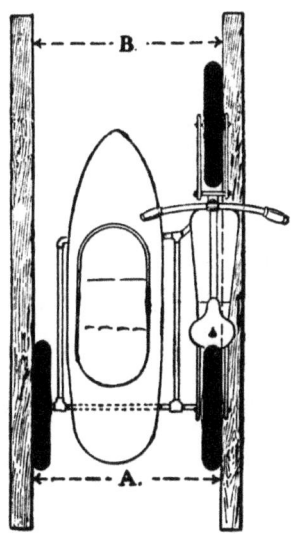

FIG. 52. CHECKING WHEEL AND SIDECAR ALIGNMENT BY MEANS OF BOARDS PLACED ALONG THE EDGES OF THE WHEELS

the wheels are in line the board should also touch both sides of the rear wheel tyre; if it does not do so the alignment of the rear wheel must be altered by means of the chain adjusters. If correct alignment cannot be obtained it is probable that the frame or forks are twisted.

Alignment of a Sidecar Machine. When lining up a combination the two wheels of the machine itself must first be checked in the manner described above. The board must then be set along the offside of the tyres and a similar board placed across the sidecar tyre as shown in Fig. 52. The distances between the boards at A and B must then be measured. In theory these distances should be equal, but, in practice, it is found that better steering is obtained if B is $\frac{3}{8}$ in. less than A.

It is next necessary to make sure that the machine itself is dead vertical. For this purpose the outfit must be wheeled on to a level surface and measurements must be taken from the front forks as shown in Fig. 53. In the sketch a piece of board is shown, but a walking stick or anything similar may well be used. The stick, or whatever is employed, should be rested against a given point on the front fork, and the distance between its lower extremity and the centre of the front tyre should then be measured. This distance is shown as *C* in Fig. 53.

A similar operation should then be carried out on the other side of the machine, and the two distances *C* should be equal. If

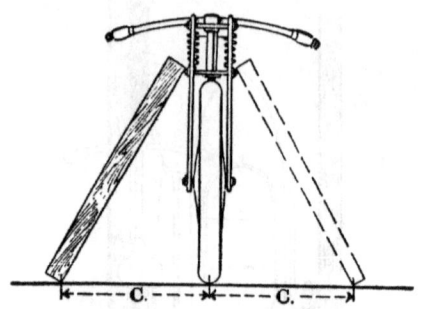

Fig. 53. If a Sidecar Machine is Vertical the Distances "C," shown Above, should be Equal

it is found that the right-hand distance *C* is greater than the left-hand, it proves that the machine is leaning towards the sidecar, and adjustments to the chassis must therefore be carried out in order that a true vertical setting may be obtained. The intelligent rider will at once know which sidecar connection must receive attention in order that the machine may be straightened. When the required adjustment has been made, the sidecar connections must be screwed up dead tight. Whether or not any alteration to the alignment is made it is advisable to check the sidecar connections from time to time.

The Matter of Tyre Pressure. As regards the tyres themselves, it is of primary importance that they should be inflated to the correct pressure. With the old type of tyre valve it was impossible to measure the pressure accurately, although expert riders could gauge it very nearly by appearance and feel.

All Ariel machines, however, are now fitted with Schrader valves and, with the aid of a pressure gauge, measurements can be taken accurately.

A chart of the minimum inflation pressures recommended for Dunlop Cord tyres fitted to Ariels is given on page 107.

It must be borne in mind that under-inflation causes severe strain to be set up in the casing of the tyre. If run at too low a pressure the casings will crack and the tyres will be rendered useless when there are still many miles of wear left in the tread. The pressures recommended are, incidentally, for machines which are normally loaded, and if the driver and passenger are very heavy, or if a pillion passenger is habitually carried, higher pressure in the rear tyre, at any rate, is advisable.

It is, again, inevitable that the tyres will become cut by the glass and sharp flints which are to be found on all our roads. A superficial cut in the rubber is of little account, but it may spread, and it should therefore be filled with a suitable tyre stopping. If, however, this cut extends to the fabric of the tyre, wet will penetrate into the latter and, in due course, will rot it. Any cut of this nature should therefore be repaired efficiently. The only way to get this done is to remove the tyre and have it vulcanized.

Obviously, if long tyre life is sought, freak hills and extremely rough surfaces should be avoided. Wheel spin in particular is extremely detrimental to the rear tyre. The majority of riders never subject their tyres to these exceptional conditions, but many of them do not appreciate the strain which they impose on their tyres by bad driving. Fierce braking, rapid acceleration and fast cornering (particularly on a sidecar machine) should be avoided as far as possible, the same applying to quick engagement of the clutch with a wide throttle opening. This latter procedure, incidentally, is also detrimental to the transmission system.

Worn Tyres and Their Danger. There is one point which solo riders in particular should remember. When a tyre is worn right through to the casing it should be treated with great care. A solo machine should never be driven at high speeds when either of its tyres is in this condition. The Dunlop tyres fitted to Ariels are of the wired-on type, and upon rapid deflation they do not leave the rim as was possible with the old pattern beaded-edge tyres. If a machine is driven at high speeds, however, and the front tyre suddenly bursts, a crash is almost inevitable. This is extremely likely if a rear tyre bursts at a speed of over 50 to 60 miles per hour, but the expert rider may be able to hold his machine and escape injury, provided that he has a clear road. A burst tyre on a sidecar machine is by no means so dangerous, but should it occur on a bend at high speed, it may cause the outfit to leave the road. If tyres, therefore, are in this badly worn condition they should be thrown away and replaced. Should the rider feel that he cannot afford this, he should drive with extreme caution and never exceed 35 to 40 miles per hour until new tyres are fitted.

For tyres to give best results they should be checked for pressure every week or fortnight, and if found to be below the recommended pressure should be inflated accordingly. At the same time they should be examined carefully throughout their circumference ; any tiny flints found embedded in the rubber should be removed, and any cuts should be repaired in the manner already described.

CHAPTER VIII

PREPARING THE ARIEL FOR COMPETITIONS

IT is essential, when a machine is being prepared for a competition of any sort, that the engine and the cycle parts should be in perfect condition. This may sound obvious, but experience has shown that it is often forgotten. The methods of getting the best from an Ariel have already been detailed in Chapter VI, and no further comments are necessary here. Let us, rather, concern ourselves with matters which are not of a mechanical nature, but which contribute largely towards success in any competitive event.

The first thing which the amateur rider must appreciate is that there are many different grades of motor-cycle competitions, and that the machine which does well in one will usually be altogether unsuitable for another. The broad heading of " competitions " covers such events as reliability trials, hill-climbs, or sprint races, sporting trials or " scrambles," and freak hill-climbs.

The Speed Element in Trials. Another point which should be understood is that almost every motor-cycle competition is, in some way or another, a race. This may sound a drastic statement, and in justification of it the different types must be considered separately. A sprint race, whether it be on the sand or road—and the latter is rare nowadays since the Auto-cycle Union has ruled that private roads only may be used for this purpose—is a race pure and simple. Most reliability trials, however, also incorporate speed tests. There are exceptions—notably some of the Motor Cycling Club's long-distance trials—but in the majority, nowadays, the premier awards go to the riders who, in addition to complying with the regulations as regards hill-climbing, time-keeping, and reliability, make the best performances in a number of special tests, prominent amongst which is the acceleration test. Most of the tests are easy, and the machine which makes the *fastest* time, consistent with its weight and size, wins the trophy.

" American " Hill-climbs. The freak hill-climb is a type of event which in the last year or so has leapt into popularity. This, again, is a race, for the winner is he who makes the fastest time of his class; but it is a race up a bumpy, grass-grown hillside, with a gradient of about 1 in 2, and skilful riding, weight distribution, and the like, play parts as important as does mere engine power. The other of the four types, the sporting trial or scramble, may not be called a race, but in most cases the scheduled speed is 20 miles per hour, whilst the course is of so arduous a nature that no one can average this speed. The *fastest* man, therefore, wins the first award, since he has lost the fewest marks.

Those who have no desire to race need not be deterred by the foregoing remarks from competing in reliability trials, at any rate. In certain trials, as already mentioned, speed plays no part

Fig. 54. The "American" Hill Climb

whatever, and in the remainder the acceleration test, although it demands terrific engine speed if premier awards are desired, calls for no exceptional riding ability. All that is required is the nerve to open the throttle fully and to let in the clutch quickly, and the ability to hold the machine as it leaps forward, and to change gear smartly and at the right moment. Before really high speeds are reached the test is finished and the rider can throttle down.

The Ordinary Reliability Test. We will consider, first, the ordinary one-day trial. In the actual riding of a machine the first-class amateur is probably as good as most trade men. He knows his mount as well as does the trade man, if not better, and he can keep his feet firmly on the rests when travelling up the worst of

PREPARING THE ARIEL FOR COMPETITIONS

freak hills. He has not, perhaps, the same chance of a premier award, for he has not the same facilities for getting speed from his engine, and he may, also, have a side-valve model from which terrific acceleration cannot be expected ; but as regards winning gold medals the two classes of rider should be equal.

Yet they are not, for in most cases the amateur has not acquired the art of trials riding. He has not studied the rules with the same concentration as has the professional, and he does the wrong thing at the wrong time. Rules and regulations differ for almost every event, and what is permissible in one trial may mean the loss of a gold medal in another. It is safe to say that the careful perusal, thorough understanding, and complete observance of the rules place the rider half-way towards a gold medal. This point cannot be over emphasised.

For the first-class performance to be made it is essential that the rider should: (1) know the course, (2) have practised the various tests, and (3) have climbed the observed hills The first of these would seem to be obvious. Route marking is never infallible, and if one man knows where he has to go and another does not, the former has a great advantage should anything go wrong with the marking. It is not, perhaps, necessary, to travel every yard of the route on the machine, but, so soon as the route card is received, the course should be traced out on a good 1 in. to the mile map, so that a thorough knowledge of its general direction is obtained.

The special tests vary in most events, the more common being acceleration, brake (sometimes combined with the acceleration test), stop and restart, and starting from cold tests. The first, as already mentioned, is usually the most important, for it is really competitive whereas, as a rule, a general standard of performance only is required for the others.

Gear Ratios. Of primary importance in the acceleration test are the gear ratios (see Chapter I), and the skilled trials rider goes to the hill whereon this test is to be held and by definite tests finds what ratios suit his machine best, allowing a margin of safety for climbing the observed hills. If the rider lives anywhere near the hill this should always be done. Should he be too far away, however, he should ascertain the gradient of the hill and time his machine on a local hill of similar gradient. The point is really important, for a gear ratio which is just right for the acceleration test may make a difference of seconds in the time. Nowadays, fortunately, there is a growing tendency amongst clubs to hold the acceleration test on the level. This is much to be preferred, since it gives the distant and the local rider equal chances.

Brake tests, as a rule, are quite simple, but when they are combined with acceleration tests, trick riding is required. In this class of test the rider usually has to accelerate from the start, stop just past a tape in the middle, run back over this tape and accelerate to the top. Over-shooting the middle tape means a great loss of time, and the best results can only be obtained from constant practice.

Practise the Stop and Restart Test. Stop and restart tests, usually held on greasy hills with severe gradients, should be practised on the actual hills for which they are scheduled, in order to make sure that the gear is low enough, the clutch sufficiently sweet, and that the back tyre will give the necessary road grip when the clutch is engaged. The last of the ordinary tests, " starting from cold," is invariably held after the lunch stop, a limit of 10 seconds or so being allowed. This test is easy to practise beforehand, but even if the machine starts easily it is advisable to surround the engine with one's coat and overalls so that it is as warm as possible when one is called upon to restart. If the machine is at all difficult to start it is usually advisable to push it off, provided that this is allowed by the rules.

Knowing an observed hill is half the battle. The hills will never actually be too steep for a well-tuned Ariel, but failure may be caused by skids or wheel-spin. Again, the hills may abound in rocks and gullies which, especially to sidecar machines, present difficulties as regards ground clearance. Therefore they should be visited and the best route up them discovered and remembered. There are many hills which are easily climbable by those who know them, but which spell failure on first acquaintance.

" Flabby " Tyres for Bad Hills. It is not generally appreciated that for climbing steep and greasy hills the tyres should have very little pressure in them. Hard tyres cause bounce, which results in skids for a solo machine and wheel-spin for a combination. Therefore, before a severe hill is reached, the tyres should be deflated until they are quite " flabby." It is not good for the tyres, but it may make the difference between success and failure in the competition. Drivers of sidecar machines, also, often find it necessary to put weight over the rear wheel to prevent spin. The trade man bolts sheets of lead on his carrier, but this is rather an expensive procedure. A simple way of keeping the back wheel down is to strap a petrol tin filled with sand and water on to the carrier, as far back as possible. The rear tyre should, of course, be practically new, and the studs on it should be as prominent as possible. Otherwise wheel-spin is sure to develop.

A sporting trial, or scramble, is a very different thing from an ordinary reliability trial, and the machine must therefore be tuned in accordance. As has already been pointed out, a scramble is usually a race, pure and simple, across open country. For the sake of appearances a 20 m.p.h. schedule is sometimes imposed, but a careful perusal of the regulations will often show that the premier award is for the fastest man, even if he should exceed the legal limit.

Nevertheless, a machine entered for a scramble should not be tuned for speed and speed alone. Rocks, water, sand, bogs, terrific up-and-down gradients, will usually have to be negotiated,

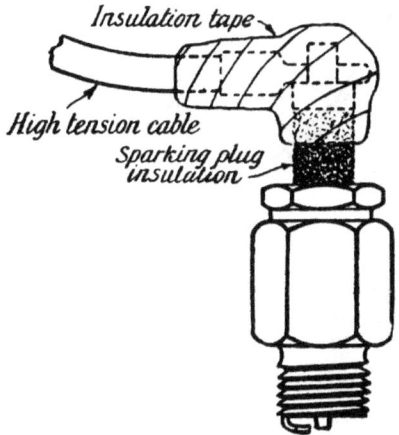

FIG. 55. FOR SPORTING TRIALS THE SPARKING PLUG TERMINAL SHOULD BE COVERED WITH INSULATION TAPE

and though speed and acceleration are required, wheel-grip and controllability are of greater value, whilst absolute reliability is more important than anything. The ideal motor-cycle for an event of this nature is one which will complete the course under its own power, non-stop.

Learning the Course. The rider must first glean some idea of the type of course to be employed in the scramble which interests him. It is usually impossible to go all round the route for, since much of it lies across open country, it cannot be followed until it is actually marked. The main obstacles, however, can sometimes be discovered and the machine can be tuned to overcome them.

It is extremely probable that deep water will have to be negotiated, and special preparations will therefore have to be made. The magneto must be coated with grease or plasticine; the sparking plug terminal must be covered with insulating tape so that the plug will fire under water (see Fig. 55); and the carburettor air-intake must be led up to a place where it is out of the way both of the actual water in the rivers and of any splash from the wheels and driving chains.

The first two points present little difficulty, but it must be remembered that a magneto will not run for ever if, by means of a coating of grease or plasticine, it is absolutely air- and watertight. Therefore the coating should be applied at the last moment before the trial, and should be removed immediately afterwards.

Waterproofing the Carburettor. A long air-intake pipe can easily be made out of a piece of car radiator hose, but it should be

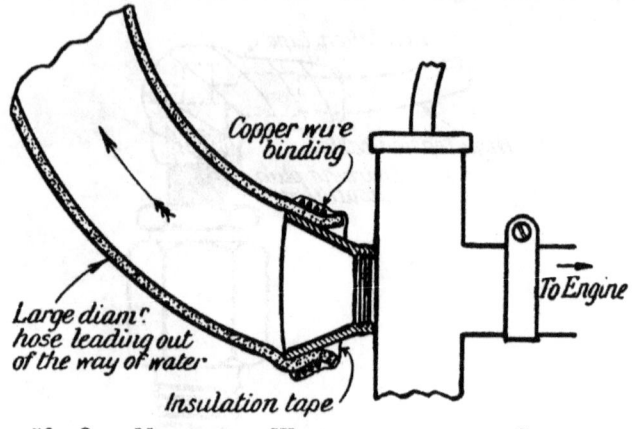

FIG. 56. ONE METHOD OF WATERPROOFING THE CARBURETTOR

arranged that this hose is of larger diameter than the actual air-intake, or carburation will be very delicate and the engine will not develop its full power. The best way to do this is to fit a metal bell-mouthed intake pipe, and fix large diameter hosing to this, making sure that the joints are secure and watertight.

Some riders think that the silencer tail pipe should also be led up out of the way of the water, but the general opinion of experienced competitors is that this is unnecessary, since the exhaust gases—of a four-stroke, at any rate—keep all the water away from the silencer, provided that the engine revolutions are kept moderately high. A disadvantage of the upraised tail pipe, also, is that should the rider fall in a water splash, water enters the silencer and the engine cannot be restarted. If one is fitted a small hole should always be drilled in the bottom of the silencer, so that any water which gets in has a draining passage. Ariel " Competition " machines have raised pipes and high-level silencers, which obviate the possibility of the entrance of water.

Attention to the Clutch. Whether mud, water, rocks, or hills are the main constituents of a sporting trial, it is certain that the

PREPARING THE ARIEL FOR COMPETITIONS

lower gears will be required constantly. The gear-box should therefore, be in perfect condition and the changes made as easy as possible. It is essential, too, that the clutch should be smooth and sound, and that it should be easy in operation; otherwise the rider will find, after an hour or so, that his left hand is powerless to work it. The clutch used on Ariels is, however, noted for its ease of action. Even more necessary in a " scramble " than in an ordinary trial are perfect brakes, correct gear ratios, a well-tuned engine which will " tick-over " as well as accelerate quickly, and a

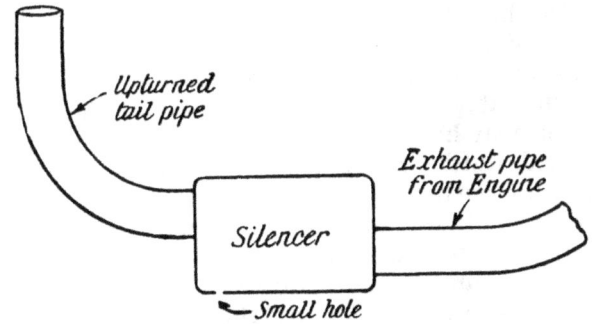

FIG. 57. IF A TURNED-UP TAIL PIPE IS USED, A SMALL DRAINAGE HOLE SHOULD BE DRILLED IN THE BOTTOM OF THE SILENCER

back tyre which will give grip on the worst of Colonial surfaces. Particular attention should therefore be paid to these points.

For freak, or American hill-climbs, there is little that can be done in the way of tuning. For these events an engine must be extremely powerful, but this is useless if the back wheel will not provide sufficient grip. More than in others, in this sort of event it is necessary to practise beforehand, so that the correct gear ratios and carburettor setting may be found. The amateur would be well advised to avoid freak hill-climbs where it is expressly stated that practising beforehand is forbidden.

Speed Events. Reliability trials, " scrambles " and freak hill-climbs have now been discussed. There remains only the speed event. It must be stated at once that side-valve Ariels are unsuitable for this class of competition.

For speed trials and hill-climbs the correct gear-ratio is even more important than it is for other competition events—it is, in fact, as important as engine efficiency. The trade rider knows this, but the amateur frequently does not, or forgets it. Indeed, it is safe to say that in an ordinary speed trial 25 per cent of the machines are hopelessly over-geared, and that a further 25 per cent would be faster were their gear-ratios lower.

Acceleration in Speed Events. The reason for this is that in speed trials there is usually either a standing start or a moderately short " flying " start. Consequently, to all intents and purposes, they are acceleration tests, and, if the gears are too high, maximum speed will not be attained until the course is almost completed, the earlier stretches having been covered at a relatively low speed. The intending rider should first ascertain the actual distance of the flying start, if a flying start is allowed. Then with a speedometer, he should repair to some safe stretch and should note how far he travels before maximum speed is obtained. He should then lower the gear and try again. Probably he will find that with the normal gear he can do, say, 80 m.p.h. ; and that although with the lower gear he can do 70 m.p.h. only, he reaches the latter speed in about 300 yd., whereas at 300 yd. on the higher gear he is doing only 60 m.p.h., the maximum not being attained until 500 or 600 yd. have been covered. Thus, over a half-mile with a short flying start, he will be much faster on time with the lower gear than he would be with the higher. The same applies when a standing start is made.

Next in importance to gear ratios is riding position. At high speeds air pressure is terrific, and the riding position, therefore, must be such that the rider can get absolutely " flat " on the tank, in order to offer as little resistance as possible. Even a T.T. position is unsuitable for sprint races, in that the rider cannot get " down to it " sufficiently. What is wanted is very low bars and a very low saddle position. Many riders, indeed, dispense with the saddle altogether and fix some sort of cushion in its place. This may be uncomfortable, but for a short race it is usually quite satisfactory. It is obvious that the lamps, horn, carrier, mudguards, etc., should be taken off, so that windage in this respect is eliminated.

Starting with a Warm Engine. The engine should, of course, be hot for the start ; otherwise much speed will be lost, owing to incomplete combustion of the gases. Again, in a short race, extra speed may be obtained by careful attention to the cycle parts. The chains, for instance, should receive a thorough wash in paraffin. The same applies to the wheel bearings, which should then be given a few drops of thin oil only. Many riders, again, balance their wheels by fixing a small weight opposite each valve, so that there is no unbalanced heavy spot on the wheels.

The gear-box before a race should be flushed out with paraffin and a very little thin oil should be inserted ; similarly, the oil supply to the engine should be cut down as much as is consistent with efficient lubrication. In every way, indeed, the machine must be tuned *for the distance.* It is only required to do half a mile or so, after which it can receive further attention before the next run, and the man who competes with his engine half full of sticky oil and his gear-box and hubs packed with thick, cold grease, is handicapping himself unnecessarily.

It should be remembered that a machine prepared in this way is not suitable for a long ride home after the event. There should be just enough oil to lubricate the cycle parts for the speed burst — and no more. As soon as the event is over, however, the gear-box, hubs, etc., should be packed with grease in the usual way.

CHAPTER IX

USEFUL INFORMATION

CYLINDER BORES AND STROKES IN MILLIMETRES AND INCHES

An Approximate Guide for Comparison

A Cylinder Measuring—	Is Equal to—
Millimetres	Inches
80 × 80	$3\frac{1}{8} \times 3\frac{1}{8}$
80 × 86	$3\frac{1}{8} \times 3\frac{3}{8}$
83 × 83	$3\frac{1}{4} \times 3\frac{1}{4}$
83 × 86	$3\frac{1}{4} \times 3\frac{3}{8}$
86 × 86	$3\frac{3}{8} \times 3\frac{3}{8}$
84 × 90	$3\frac{5}{16} \times 3\frac{6}{16}$
90 × 90	$3\frac{9}{16} \times 3\frac{9}{16}$
90 × 110	$3\frac{9}{16} \times 4\frac{5}{16}$
95 × 115	$3\frac{3}{4} \times 4\frac{6}{14}$
100 × 115	$3\frac{15}{16} \times 4\frac{9}{16}$
105 × 118	$4\frac{1}{8} \times 4\frac{5}{8}$
108 × 120	$4\frac{1}{4} \times 4\frac{3}{4}$
110 × 125	$4\frac{5}{16} \times 4\frac{15}{16}$
112 × 128	$4\frac{7}{16} \times 5\frac{1}{16}$
114 × 130	$4\frac{1}{2} \times 5\frac{1}{8}$
116 × 134	$4\frac{9}{16} \times 5\frac{5}{16}$
118 × 138	$4\frac{5}{8} \times 5\frac{7}{16}$
120 × 140	$4\frac{3}{4} \times 5\frac{1}{2}$
122 × 143	$4\frac{3}{16} \times 5\frac{5}{8}$
124 × 146	$4\frac{7}{8} \times 5\frac{3}{4}$
126 × 148	$4\frac{15}{16} \times 5\frac{3}{8}$
128 × 150	$5\frac{1}{16} \times 5\frac{15}{16}$

FORMULAE FOR H.P.

S = Stroke in centimetres
D = Diameter of cylinder in centimetres
R = Revolutions per minute
N = Number of cylinders

R.A.C. Formula H.P. $= \dfrac{D^2 \times N}{16 \cdot 13}$

A.C.U. Formula = 100 c.c. = 1 h.p.

A more accurate formula is the Dendy Marshall, in which—

$$\text{H.P.} = \frac{D^2 \times S \times N \times R}{200{,}000}$$

TYRE PRESSURES

Model	26 in. × 3 in. Lb. per sq. in.			26 in. × 3·25 in. Lb. per sq. in.			26 in. × 3·50 in. Lb. per sq. in.			25 in. × 3 in. Lb. per sq. in.		25 in. × 3·25 in. Lb. per sq. in.	
	Front	Rear	Sidecar	Front	Rear	Sidecar	Front	Rear	Sidecar	Front	Rear	Front	Rear
SB, SG, 4F:													
Solo . .	—	—	—	17	23	—	16	19	—	—	—	—	—
Sidecar . .	—	—	—	21	31	16	17	27	16	—	—	—	—
VB, VG, VH:													
Solo . .	17	—	—	16	21	—	16	17	—	—	—	—	—
Sidecar . .	—	—	—	19	28	16	16	24	16	—	—	—	—
LB, LF, MB, MF, MH:													
Solo . .	16	19	—	—	—	—	—	—	—	18	25	16	19

TYRE SIZE EQUIVALENTS

65 Millimetres	=	2½ in.	650 Millimetres	=	26 in.
80 „	=	3 „	700 „	=	28 „
85 „	=	3¼ „	750 „	=	30 „
90 „	=	3½ „	800 „	=	32 „
100 „	=	4 „	870 „	=	34 „
105 „	=	4¼ „	910 „	=	36 „
120 „	=	5 „	1010 „	=	40 „

INTERNATIONAL MARKS

An oval plate is used, the distinguishing marks of the country of origin, consisting of one or two letters, painted in black upon a white ground.

A	Austria	GB	Gt. Britain & Ireland	NL	The Netherlands
B	Belgium	GR	Greece	P	Portugal
BG	Bulgaria	H	Hungary	R	Russia
CH	Switzerland	I	Italy	RM	Rumania
D	Germany	MC	Monaco	S	Sweden
E	Spain	MN	Montenegro	SB	Servia
F	France	CS	Czecho Slovakia	US	U.S.A.

INDEX

ACCIDENTS, what to do, 25
Alignment of sidecar, 93
Ariel sidecars, 15
Automatic traffic indicators, 36

BRAKE, internal construction, 5

CARBURETTOR, 42
——, waterproofing, 102
Clutch, attention to, 54
——, use of, 33

DANGER signs, 36
Decarbonizing, 60
Depreciation, 19
Driving licence, 24

FOUR-stroke principle, 39
Frame construction, 5

GAP of plugs, 51
Gear box, 4
—— ratios, 17

INSURANCE, 26

KICK-starting, 31

LIGHTING regulations, 27
Lubrication system, 2

MAGNETO, care of, 89
—— timing, 81
Mileage costs, 23

NUMBER-plate dimensions, 27
New motor laws, 25

OIL consumption, 20
—— regulator, 32
Overhead rocker box, 60
Overhead valves, dismantling, 70

PILLION riding, 30
Piston rings, 68
Petrol consumption, 20
Plug testing, 51
Police and motor-cyclists, 25
Premiums, insurance, 20

RANGE of Ariels, 1
Removing valves, 70
Renewing a driving licence, 24
Road signs, 35
Rocker arm, 60
Running costs, 18
—— -in engine, 31

SKIDDING, 34
Sports sidecar, 16
Spring forks, 5
Steering damper, 33
Sparking plug, 51

TANK of Ariel machines, 13
Tappet adjustment, 48
Timing gear, 76
—— magneto, 81
Tyre pressure, 94
Tyres, life of, 95

VALVE gear, 70
—— grinding, 72

WATERPROOFING carburettor, 102
Wheels, care of, 92
Worn tyres, danger of, 95

VELOCEPRESS MANUALS - MOTORCYCLE

1930'S BRITISH MOTORCYCLE CARBS & ELEC COMPONENTS (BOOK OF)
1930'S BRITISH MOTORCYCLE ENGINES (OVERHAUL & MAINTENANCE)
1930'S BRITISH MOTORCYCLE GEARBOXES & CLUTCHES (BOOK OF)
AJS 1932-1948 SINGLES & TWINS 250cc THRU 1000cc (BOOK OF)
AJS 1945-1960 SINGLES 350cc & 500cc MODELS 16 & 18 (BOOK OF)
AJS 1955-1965 SINGLES 350cc & 500cc (BOOK OF)
ARIEL UP TO 1932 (BOOK OF)
ARIEL 1932-1939 PREWAR MODELS (BOOK OF)
ARIEL 1933-1951 (WORKSHOP MANUAL)
ARIEL 1939-1960 4 STROKE SINGLES (BOOK OF)
ARIEL 1958-1964 LEADER & ARROW (BOOK OF)
BMW R26 R27 (1956-1967) FACTORY WORKSHOP MANUAL
BMW R50 R50S R60 R69S (1955-1969) FACTORY WORKSHOP MANUAL
BRIDGESTONE 90 SERIES FACTORY WSM & PARTS CATALOGUE
BRIDGESTONE 175 SERIES FACTORY WSM & PARTS CATALOGUE
BSA BANTAM ALL MODELS FROM 1948 ONWARDS (BOOK OF)
BSA SINGLES & V-TWINS UP TO 1927 (BOOK OF)
BSA SINGLES & V-TWINS UP TO 1935 (BOOK OF)
BSA SINGLES & V-TWINS 1936-1939 (BOOK OF)
BSA SINGLES & V-TWINS 1936-1952 (BOOK OF)
BSA OHV & SV SINGLES 250-600cc 1945-1954 (BOOK OF)
BSA OHV & SV SINGLES 250cc 1954-1970 (BOOK OF)
BSA OHV SINGLES 350 & 500cc 1955-1967 (BOOK OF)
BSA TWINS 1948-1962 (BOOK OF)
BSA TWINS 1962-1969 (SECOND BOOK OF)
CYCLEMOTOR (BOOK OF)
DOUGLAS 1929-1939 PREWAR ALL MODELS (BOOK OF)
DOUGLAS 1948-1957 POSTWAR ALL MODELS FACTORY SHOP MANUAL
DUCATI 160cc, 250cc & 350cc OHC MODELS FACTORY WORKSHOP MANUAL
HONDA 50 ALL MODELS UP TO 1970 INC MONKEY & TRAIL (BOOK OF)
HONDA 90 ALL MODELS UP TO 1966 (BOOK OF)
HONDA 125-150cc TWINS C/CS/CB/CA FACTORY WORKSHOP MANUAL
HONDA 250-305 TWINS C/CS/CB FACTORY WORKSHOP MANUAL
HONDA C100 SUPER CUB FACTORY WORKSHOP MANUAL
HONDA C110 SPORT CUB 1962-1969 FACTORY WORKSHOP MANUAL
HONDA TWINS & SINGLES 50cc THRU 305cc 1960-1966 (BOOK OF)
HONDA TWINS ALL MODELS 125cc THRU 450cc UP TO 1968 (BOOK OF)
J.A.P. ENGINES 1927-1952 & MOTORCYCLES 1934-1952 (BOOK OF)
LAMBRETTA 1947-1957 ALL 125 & 150cc MODELS (BOOK OF)
LAMBRETTA 1957-1970 LI & TV MODELS (SECOND BOOK OF)
MATCHLESS 1931-1939 ALL MODELS 250cc THRU 990cc (BOOK OF)
MATCHLESS 1945-1956 350 & 500cc SINGLES (BOOK OF)
MATCHLESS 1955-1966 350 & 500cc SINGLES (BOOK OF)
NEW IMPERIAL ALL SV & OHV FROM 1935 ONWARDS (BOOK OF)
NORTON 1932-1939 PREWAR MODELS (BOOK OF)
NORTON 1932-1947 (BOOK OF)
NORTON 1938-1956 (BOOK OF)
NORTON 1955-1963 MODELS 19, 50 & ES2 (BOOK OF)
NORTON 1955-1965 DOMINATOR TWINS (BOOK OF)
NORTON 1957-1970 TWINS FACTORY WORKSHOP MANUAL
NSU PRIMA 1956-1964 ALL MODELS (BOOK OF)
NSU QUICKLY 1953-1963 ALL MODELS (BOOK OF)
PANTHER 1932-1958 LIGHTWEIGHT MODELS 250 & 350cc (BOOK OF)
PANTHER 1938-1966 HEAVYWEIGHT MODELS 600 & 650cc (BOOK OF)
RALEIGH MOPEDS 1960-1969 (BOOK OF)
RALEIGH MOTORCYCLES 1919-1933 (BOOK OF)
ROYAL ENFIELD 1934-1946 SINGLES & V TWINS (BOOK OF)
ROYAL ENFIELD 1937-1953 SINGLES & V TWINS (BOOK OF)
ROYAL ENFIELD 1946-1962 SINGLES (BOOK OF)
ROYAL ENFIELD 1958-1966 250cc & 350cc SINGLES (SECOND BOOK OF)
ROYAL ENFIELD 736cc INTERCEPTOR FACTORY WORKSHOP MANUAL
RUDGE 1933-1939 (BOOK OF)
SUNBEAM 1928-1939 (BOOK OF)
SUNBEAM 1946-1957 S7 & S8 (BOOK OF)
SUZUKI 50cc & 80cc UP TO 1966 (BOOK OF)
SUZUKI T10 1963-1967 FACTORY WORKSHOP MANUAL
SUZUKI T20 & T200 1965-1969 FACTORY WORKSHOP MANUAL
TRIUMPH 1935-1939 PREWAR MODELS (BOOK OF)
TRIUMPH 1935-1949 (BOOK OF)
TRIUMPH 1937-1951 (WORKSHOP MANUAL)
TRIUMPH 1945-1955 FACTORY WORKSHOP MANUAL
TRIUMPH 1945-1958 TWINS (BOOK OF)
TRIUMPH 1956-1969 TWINS (BOOK OF)
VELOCETTE 1925-1970 ALL SINGLES & TWINS (BOOK OF)
VESPA 1951-1961 (BOOK OF)
VESPA 1955-1963 125 & 150cc & GS MODELS (SECOND BOOK OF)
VESPA 1955-1968 GS & SS (BOOK OF)
VESPA 1963-1972 90, 125 & 150cc (THIRD BOOK OF)
VILLIERS ENGINE UP TO 1959 INC. 3 WHEELERS (BOOK OF)
VILLIERS ENGINE UP TO 1969 (BOOK OF)
VINCENT 1935-1955 (WORKSHOP MANUAL)

VELOCEPRESS TECHNICAL BOOKS – MOTORCYCLE

CATALOG OF BRITISH MOTORCYCLES (1951 MODELS)
INDIAN PONYBIKE, BOY RACER & PAPOOSE ILL PARTS LIST & SALES LIT
MOTORCYCLE ENGINEERING (P.E. Irving)
SPEED AND HOW TO OBTAIN IT (Motor Cycle Magazine UK)
TUNING FOR SPEED (P.E. Irving)

VELOCEPRESS MANUALS - THREE WHEELER'S

BSA THREE WHEELER (BOOK OF)
VINTAGE MORGAN THREE WHEELER (BOOK OF)

VELOCEPRESS MANUALS - AUTOMOBILE

ALFA ROMEO GIULIA WORKSHOP MANUAL 1300 TO 2000cc 1962-1975
ALFA ROMEO GIULIA TECH MANUAL CARBURETED CARS FROM 1962
ALFA ROMEO GIULIA TECH MANUAL FUEL INJECTED CARS FROM 1969
AUSTIN-HEALEY 6-CYLINDER WORKSHOP MANUAL
AUSTIN-HEALEY SPRITE & MG MIDGET WORKSHOP MANUAL 1958-1971
BMW 600 LIMOUSINE FACTORY WORKSHOP MANUAL
BMW 600 LIMOUSINE OWNERS HAND BOOK & SERVICE MANUAL
BMW 2000 & 2002 1966-1976 WORKSHOP MANUAL
BMW ISETTA FACTORY WORKSHOP MANUAL
CORVAIR 1960-1969 WORKSHOP MANUAL
CORVETTE V8 1955-1962 WORKSHOP MANUAL
FIAT 500 FACTORY WORKSHOP MANUAL 1957-1973
FIAT 600, 600D & MULTIPLA FACTORY WORKSHOP MANUAL 1955-1969
JAGUAR E-TYPE 3.8 & 4.2 SERIES 1 & 2 WORKSHOP MANUAL
JAGUAR MK 7, 8, 9 & XK120, 140, 150 WORKSHOP MANUAL 1948-1961
METROPOLITAN FACTORY WORKSHOP MANUAL
MGA & MGB OWNERS HANDBOOK & WORKSHOP MANUAL
MG MIDGET TC, TD, TF & TF1500 WORKSHOP MANUAL
PORSCHE 356 1948-1965 WORKSHOP MANUAL
PORSCHE 911 2.0, 2.2, 2.4 LITRE 1964-1973
PORSCHE 912 WORKSHOP MANUAL
TRIUMPH TR2, TR3, TR4 1953-1965 WORKSHOP MANUAL
VOLKSWAGEN TRANSPORTER, TRUCKS & WAGONS 1950-1979 WSM
VOLVO 1944-1968 ALL MODELS WORKSHOP MANUAL

VELOCEPRESS TECHNICAL BOOKS - AUTOMOBILE

FERRARI 250/GT SERVICE AND MAINTENANCE
FERRARI GUIDE TO PERFORMANCE
FERRARI OWNER'S HANDBOOK
FERRARI TUNING TIPS & MAINTENANCE TECHNIQUES
HOW TO BUILD A FIBERGLASS CAR
HOW TO BUILD A RACING CAR
HOW TO RESTORE THE MODEL 'A' FORD
MASERATI OWNER'S HANDBOOK
OBERT'S FIAT GUIDE
PERFORMANCE TUNING THE SUNBEAM TIGER
SOUPING THE VOLKSWAGEN
SOLEX CARBURETORS (EMPHASIS ON UK & EU AUTOMOBILES)
SU CARBURETORS (EMPHASIS ON UK AUTOMOBILES)
WEBER CARBURETORS (EMPHASIS ON ALFA & FIAT)

VELOCEPRESS BOOKS & GUIDES - AUTOMOBILE

ABARTH BUYERS GUIDE
COMPLETE CATALOG OF JAPANESE MOTOR VEHICLES
FERRARI 308 SERIES BUYER'S AND OWNER'S GUIDE
FERRARI BERLINETTA LUSSO
FERRARI BROCHURES AND SALES LITERATURE 1946-1967
FERRARI BROCHURES AND SALES LITERATURE 1968-1989
FERRARI OPP, MAINTENANCE & SERVICE H/BOOKS 1948-1963
FERRARI SERIAL NUMBERS PART I - ODD NUMBERS TO 21399
FERRARI SERIAL NUMBERS PART II - EVEN NUMBERS TO 1050
FERRARI SPYDER CALIFORNIA
HENRY'S FABULOUS MODEL "A" FORD
MASERATI BROCHURES AND SALES LITERATURE

VELOCEPRESS BOOKS – RACING

CARRERA PANAMERICANA - MEXICAN ROAD RACE (BOOK OF)
DIALED IN - THE JAN OPPERMAN STORY
IF HEMINGWAY HAD WRITTEN A RACING NOVEL
VEDA ORR'S NEW REVISED HOT ROD PICTORIAL

AUTOBOOKS WORKSHOP MANUALS & BROOKLANDS ROAD TEST PORTFOLIOS

FOR A COMPLETE LISTING OF THE AUTOBOOKS & BROOKLANDS TITLES THAT WE CURRENTLY HAVE AVAILABLE, PLEASE VISIT OUR WEBSITE.

For a detailed description of any of the titles listed above please visit our website

www.VelocePress.com

www.ingramcontent.com/pod-product-compliance
Lightning Source LLC
Chambersburg PA
CBHW070558170426
43201CB00012B/1877